Accessible Wales
A Disabled Visitor's Guide

CW01266052

Contents

Published by Wales Council for the Disabled in association with the Wales Tourist Board

Compiled by: Jay Ashton

Accommodation section compiled by: Wales Tourist Board

Edited by: Howard John, Alison Williams and Roger Thomas

Copyright © 1991   ISBN NO. 1 85013 0450

Chairman's Foreword

Croeso i Gymru! Our 'Welcome to Wales' is a warm and practical one. We hope that this publication will be of help to you in finding what is available in Wales. The Wales Council for the Disabled is committed to improving the understanding of disability and the easing of access everywhere.

It is several years since we published the first visitor's guide and we have been able to add to and update our information. We have been helped in this by the Wales Tourist Board, and thank them and the advertisers for the support they have given us. We hope that as facilities improve and we learn of these that we can produce further editions. We will be glad of your help in this by your advice and comment on how we can make the guide more useful to you and whether you are coming to Wales to visit us, or already live here and want to know what facilities exist for people with disabilities.

Pob hwyl! Enjoy your stay in Wales.
John Ashton Edwards
Chairman, Wales Council for the Disabled.

Rhagair Y Cadeirydd

Croeso i Gymru! Mae'n croeso yn un cynnes ac ymarfarol. Rydym yn gobeithio y bydd y cyhoeddiad hwn o gymorth i chi i ddarganfod yr hyn sydd ar gael yng Nghymru. Mae Cyngor Cymru i'r Anabl yn ymroi i wella dealltwriaeth o anabledd a hwyluso hygyrchedd ym mhobman. Mae llawer blwyddyn wedi mynd heibio ers i ni gyhoeddi'r canllaw cyntaf i ymwelwyr ac rydym wedi gallu ychwanegu at, a diweddaru'n gwybodaeth. Rydym wedi cael cymorth i wneud hyn gan Fwrdd Croeso Cymru, ac yn diolch iddynt hwy a'u hysbysebwyr am y gefnogaeth rydym wedi ei derbyn oddi wrthynt. Rydym yn gobeithio y gallwn gynhyrchu argraffiadau pellach wrth i gyfleusterau wella ac i ni ddod yn ymwybodol o chonynt. Byddwn yn falch hefyd o gael eich cymorth chi yn hyn o beth drwy dderbyn eich cyngor a'ch sylwadau ar y ffordd y gallem wneud y canllaw yn fwy defnyddiol i chi a ph'un a ydych yn dod i Gymru i ymweld â ni, neu'n byw yma eisoes ac yn awyddus i wybod pa gyfleusterau sy'n bodoli i bobl gydag anableddau.

Pob hwyl! Mwynhewch eich arhosiad yng Nghymru.
John Ashton Edwards
Cadeirydd, Cyngor Cymru i'r Anabl

Accessible Wales

No one can pretend that it is easy for disabled visitors. Disabled people have, for too long, faced many problems when travelling, ranging from poorly designed buildings to unhelpful staff attitudes. In recent years, things have started to change for the better, not only in Wales but throughout Britain. This guide is designed to help you find the increasing number of facilities that *are* accessible in Wales.

In recent years more buildings, public spaces and services have been opened up and many more places to stay, tourist attractions, theatres, sports centres, community facilities and even countryside activities are now accessible to disabled people. *Accessible Wales* lists a wide range of such services, facilities and activities.

With over 379,000 disabled people, Wales has the highest level of disability in Britain. In addition, many disabled visitors spend time here each year on business, for a short break or a longer holiday. A change in attitude to disability on the part of politicians and planners is of crucial concern to any disabled person - local and visitor alike - who wants to get out and about in this beautiful country.

As you will see from the contents of this guide, the trend is in the right direction. Wales is much better equipped today to welcome disabled visitors than ever before. And, as more disabled visitors use facilities, so the awareness of the problems faced by such travellers will spread. *Accessible Wales* will point you in the right direction. Its contents reflect the work that the Wales Tourist Board, National Trust, local authorities, other government bodies and helpful individuals are engaged in to make Wales's attractive coastline and countryside accessible to all.

Caernarfon Castle.

Using this guide

Accessible Wales is not a comprehensive directory to *every* accessible facility in Wales. But we have tried to include at least one example of what is available locally under various headings in each part of Wales. So wherever you travel in Wales, you will have information on where to stay, where to go, things to do, and the basic facilities everyone needs.

We have tried to be honest and accurate, but perhaps in some cases you may find our assessments *too* pessimistic - or optimistic. It is difficult to assess tourist facilities with everyone's needs in mind. We are all different and only you know exactly what you are looking for.

Wherever possible, we have included a telephone number. The Wales Council for the Disabled recommends that you telephone ahead if possible, not just to check if the facilities are suitable, but also to confirm that they are available *when* you want. Even the best-designed facilities get booked up or put out of action.

This guide is divided into five main sections

1 ● **Getting around**
Transport services in Wales;

2 ● **Where to stay**
A list of hotels and self-catering accommodation assessed for standards and accessibility by Wales Tourist Board verification officers;

3 ● **Things to do**
A wide range of places to visit and leisure activities;

4 ● **Local facilities**
Lists of places to eat and drink, banks and post offices, toilets and other essential facilities;

5 ● **In emergencies**
A directory of essential health and equipment services.

The *Where to Stay* section is divided into North, Mid and South Wales, while every other section is divided into *county* entries and facilities are listed in *alphabetical* order. The map at the back of this guide shows main towns and sites.

Arranging your visit

The following guidelines may be useful, especially if you are travelling independently.

★ **Do not travel alone unless you are confident that you will not need assistance.**

★ **Find out as much as possible about the area(s) you will be visiting.**

★ **Plan ahead, telephone ahead.**

★ **When contacting accommodation, restaurants, etc., be honest about your needs. Your check list might include ramps, steps, parking, room location, handrails, hoists and other equipment, transport facilities, communication aids, access to lifts, bedrooms, bathrooms, etc.**

★ **If you are going on holiday, check insurance cover.**

★ **Take spare equipment, repair kits, etc.**

★ **Take sufficient supplies of any medicines.**

Free information and advice on planning your holiday can be provided by the Holiday Care Service at 2 Old Bank Chambers, Station Road, Horley, Surrey RH6 9HW. Tel: (0293) 774535.

The number, type and quality of facilities for disabled visitors in Wales is increasing. You can help by:

★ *using* **available facilities;**

★ *complaining* **when things aren't right;**

★ *letting us know* **at the Wales Council for the Disabled of any facility, good or bad, that you have used in Wales, using the return form at the back of the book.**

Perhaps one day there will be no need for guides such as this. perhaps one day we will be able to travel in the safe assumption that everything we would like to do and everywhere we would like to go is accessible. Until then, we hope you find this guide to *Accessible Wales* **useful - and** *Croeso i Gymru, Welcome to Wales!*

IS PROUD TO
S·U·P·P·O·R·T

. . . . The Wales Council for the Disabled

Cambrian Coast

Getting around:

Travelling in Wales

Many people are attracted to Wales because of the immense variety and quality of its scenery. But Wales's mountain ranges, hills, valleys, rivers and rugged seashores present a challenge to providers of public transport. While the coastal areas of South and North Wales are served with reasonably good rail and road links, getting around the rest of Wales using public transport does present problems for disabled people. The best way to travel is by car. Here, the picture is different. Wales has an excellent road network, so access to main holiday resorts and off-the-beaten-track locations should present few problems to disabled travellers.

Public Transport

By Bus

Few bus operators in Wales run regular services accessible to wheelchair users.

By Taxi

Some local authorities are beginning to look at accessible taxi services. Cardiff, for example, is taking the lead by introducing 25 new licences for wheelchair accessible taxis and mandatory disability awareness training for taxi drivers.

By Rail

Mainline services into South and North Wales from Britain's main centres of population are good (London to Cardiff takes only 1 hour 45 minutes, for example) and there are branch lines which travel through parts of Mid Wales. An increasing number of unstaffed and inaccessible stations, though, does present problems for anyone with mobility difficulties wishing to travel by rail.

The following principal stations claim to be accessible, though it is always advisable to telephone ahead to ensure that the facilities you need are available. Please contact the customer services department at any of the three numbers listed below.

Cardiff: Tel (0222) 499811
Chester: Tel (0244) 346737
Swansea: Tel (0792) 650808

The following stations are accessible to disabled visitors.

CLWYD:
Colwyn Bay, Rhyl, Wrexham General.

DYFED:
Aberystwyth, Carmarthen, Haverfordwest, Llanelli.

MID GLAMORGAN:
Caerphilly, Merthyr Tydfil, Rhymney.

SOUTH GLAMORGAN:
Cardiff Central.

WEST GLAMORGAN:
Swansea.

GWENT:
Newport.

GWYNEDD:
Bangor, Blaenau Ffestiniog, Porthmadog.

POWYS:
Machynlleth.

The Wales Council for the Disabled has conducted an access survey of British Rail stations in Wales. For details of local stations, contact the Council's Access Unit.

By Air

Wales has two airports.

● *Cardiff-Wales Airport.*
Tel: (0446) 711111
Wheelchair lift and accessible WC, stair lift from international departure lounges.

● *Caernarfon Airport.*
Tel: (0286) 830800
Special facilities; accessible WC.

By Sea

Sealink, the B&I Line and Swansea-Cork Ferries operate Irish Sea ferry services. Operators will make every effort to assist disabled passengers. Please contact them in advance to make suitable arrangements.

The ferries run between the following ports:

Fishguard to Rosslare (Sealink)
Pembroke to Rosslare (B & I)
Swansea to Cork (Swansea-Cork Ferries)
Holyhead to Dun Laoghaire (Sealink UK)
Holyhead to Dublin (B&I)

Access is good at both the Holyhead and Pembroke terminals, though tidal effects can mean that an ordinary gangplank has to be used occasionally at Holyhead.

Please contact:
B&I Line, Reliance House, Water Street, Liverpool L2 8TP. Tel: (051) 227 3131.
Sealink UK Ltd, Charter House, Park Street, Ashford, Kent TN24 8EX. Tel: (0233) 647022.
Swansea-Cork Ferries, Swansea Dock, Swansea, West Glamorgan. Tel: (0792) 456116.

Private Transport

By Car

For most people, the only feasible way of travelling around Wales is by car. One of the common problems facing non-ambulant disabled drivers is the ubiquitous self-service petrol station. The following petrol stations have forecourt service or staff assistance.

CLWYD

●*Abergele:*
Richmond Garage, Towyn. Tel (0745) 825794.
●*Colwyn Bay:*
Expressway, Llandulas. Tel (0492) 512110.
Gwyns Service Station, Conway Road, Mochdre. Tel (0492) 46617.
●*Deeside:*
Northop Garage, Ewloe. Tel (0244) 542766.
●*Holywell:*
Hillcrest Motor Co., Halkin Road. Tel (0352) 711711.
●*Rhyl:*
Heron Service Station, Coast Road. Tel (0745) 344374.
●*Wrexham:*
Erddig Motors, Chester Road, LL12 8DY. Tel (0744) 57033.

DYFED

●*Aberaeron:*
Aeron Coast Service Station, Caravan Park, North Road. Tel (0545) 570649.

●*Aberystwyth:*
Aberystwyth Service Station, Mill Street.
Tel (0970) 615244.

●*Begelly:*
Crossroads Garage. Tel (0834) 812276.

●*Carmarthen:*
Tanerdy Garage, Tanerdy. Tel (0267) 236203.

●*Clynderwen:*
Tyssul Garage, Glandy Cross. Tel (0994) 7230.

●*Eglwyswrw:*
Penfro Service Station. Tel (0239) 79618.

●*Haverfordwest:*
Ridgeway Service Station, Fishguard Road.
Tel (0437) 2228.

●*Johnstone:*
Haverfordwest Garage, St Peters Road,
Tel (0437) 890038.

●*Lampeter:*
D.D. Evans Garage, North Road.
Tel (0570) 422549.

●*Llandeilo:*
Manordeilo Garage. Tel (0554) 777374.

●*Llandysul:*
Valley Services, Pencader Road.
Tel (0559) 322288.

●*Llanelli:*
Halletts Service Station, Pottery Street.
Tel (0554) 755206.
Heron Service Station, Cross Hands.
Tel (0269) 845848.

●*Newgale:*
Newgale Service Station. Tel (0437) 721398.

●*St Clears:*
Carmarthen Road Service Station.
Tel (0994) 230153.

●*Saundersfoot:*
Old Pump Service Station, Pentlepoir.
Tel (0834) 812359.

●*Whitland:*
Cambrian Auto Co. Tel (0994) 240420.

MID GLAMORGAN

●*Aberdare:*
Golden Acres Service Station, Park View
Terrace, Abercwmboi. Tel (0443) 427380.

●*Caerphilly:*
Bedwas Road Filling Station, Bedwas Road.
Tel (0222) 882830.

●*Merthyr Tydfil:*
Thomas & Davies, Pentrebach Road.
Tel (0685) 722773.

●*Porth:*
Trebanog Service Station, Trebanog Road,
Rhondda. Tel (0443) 682109.

●*Taffs Well:*
Halfway Garage, Cardiff Road.
Tel (0222) 810535.

●*Tonypandy:*
Tonypandy Petrol Station, Llwynypia.
Tel (0443) 432814.

●*Trethomas:*
Heron Service Station, (A468).

SOUTH GLAMORGAN

●*Cardiff:*
Cardiff Garage, Caerphilly Road.
Tel (0222) 621751.
Howells Motors, 501 Newport Road.
Tel (0222) 855392.

WEST GLAMORGAN

●*Amman Valley:*
Park Garage, Brynaman. Tel (0269) 822293.

●*Pontardawe:*
Trebanos Petrol Station, 142/146 Swansea
Road, Trebanos. Tel (0792) 863686.

●*Swansea:*
Abertawe Service Station, 1093 Carmarthen
Road, Fforestfach. Tel (0792) 586129.
Halfway Garage, Mumbles Road, Blackpill.
Tel (0792) 203451.
Sketty Petrol Station, 76/78 Gower Road,
Sketty. Tel (0792) 204800.

GWENT

●*Newport:*
Highcross Garage, High Cross Road,
Rogerstone. Tel (0633) 892712.
Malpas Service Station, Malpas Road,
Newport. Tel (0633) 858057.

We care so much for our disabled customers, we've written a book about it.

British Telecom's guide
to equipment and services
for disabled customers

TELECOM

At British Telecom Wales and the Marches we are concerned that all our customers should get the best possible service at all times.

That's why we offer a wide selection of phones in a variety of different sizes, shapes and styles; all designed to be as easy to use as possible.

However, although our standard range covers most people's requirements, we are aware that some of our customers have special problems using the phone.

To help them we have produced a booklet showing the ways in which our disabled and elderly customers can derive greater benefit from our wide range of products and services. This includes a number of special aids to help overcome the problems experienced by people with impaired sight, hearing, speech or mobility.

For more details or for a free copy of British Telecom's guide to equipment and services dial 100 and ask for **Freefone BT Disabled.**

British
T̈ELECOM

Wales and the Marches

●*Pontllanfraith:*
Sirhowy Service Station, Commercial Street.
Tel (0495) 223344.

●*Pontypool:*
Heron Service Station, (A4042), New Inn,
Pontymoile. Tel (0495) 752112.
Pimlico Garage, New Inn. Tel (0495) 553737.

●*Tredegar:*
Tredegar Service Station, Sirhowy Bridge,
Beaufort Road. Tel (0495) 252760.

GWYNEDD

●*Anglesey:*
Britannia Garage, Menai Bridge.
Tel (0248) 712373.
Four Crosses Service Station, Amlwch
Road, Menai Bridge. Tel (0248) 712353.
Glen Cottage Service Station, London
Road, Gwalchmai. Tel (0407) 720525.
Parry Davies & Co., Land's End,
Holyhead. Tel (0248) 714335.

●*Betws-y-Coed:*
Waterloo Bridge Service Station,
Holyhead Road. Tel (0690) 2305.

●*Caernarfon:*
Lleiod Garage, Llanberis Road. Tel (0286)
3249.

●*Conwy:*
Castle Garage, The Mart. Tel (0492) 592498.

●*Deganwy:*
Black Cat Filling Station, Glan Conwy
Corner. Tel (0492) 581174.

●*Llandudno:*
Promenade Garage. Tel (0492) 76795.
West Shore Garage, Herkomer Street,
West Shore. Tel (0492) 77607.

●*Llanrwst:*
Jones Bros', Kerry Garage, Plough Street.
Tel (0492) 640381.

●*Penmaenmawr:*
Glyn Percin Garage, Conwy Old Road.
Tel (0492) 623303.
Orme View Service Station, Conway Road.
Tel (0492) 622741.

●*Porthmadog:*
Harbour Service Station, High Street.
Tel (0766) 512716.

POWYS

●*Newtown:*
W R Davies Motors, Pool Road.
Tel (0686) 25514.

●*Welshpool:*
Border Garage, Newtown Road.
Tel (0938) 4444.

MOTORWAY SERVICE STATIONS (M4)
CARDIFF WEST (Rank): Junction 33
SARN PARK (Welcome Break): Junction 36
PONT ABRAHAM (Road Chef): Junction 49

Mawddach Estuary

Where to stay

Wales has a wide range of holiday accommodation

Everything from country house hotels to guest houses, traditional resort hotels to self-catering, inns to caravan holiday home parks.

The Wales Tourist Board is actively encouraging the provision of disabled facilities in holiday accommodation. The following list of suitable accommodation for disabled guests has been compiled by official verification officers who visited each property to check facilities. All properties have also been verified, which means that they have to conform to certain standards (many, of course, will offer very high standards of accommodation).

The Wales Council for the Disabled recommends that you telephone accommodation ahead if possible, not just to check if the facilities are suitable, but also to confirm that they are available *when* you want.

The following list, divided into hotels, guest houses, self-catering, caravan holiday home parks, touring caravan parks, camping sites and youth hostels, grades the access for disabled people. The grades, ranging from 1 - 3, are based on the following criteria:

ACCESS GRADE 1   *Premises accessible to a wheelchair user travelling independently.*

ACCESS GRADE 2   *Premises accessible to a wheelchair user travelling with assistance.*

ACCESS GRADE 3   *Premises accessible to someone with mobility difficulties but able to walk a few paces and up to a maximum of 3 steps.*

NORTH WALES ACCOMMODATION

HOTELS

BANGOR

The British Hotel

High Street, Bangor, Gwynedd
LL57 1NP
Contact: Mr C V Jones
Tel (0248) 364911
Access Grade **2**

BEAUMARIS

Bulkeley Arms

Castle Street, Beaumaris, Gwynedd
LL58 8AP
Contact: Mr Rhodes
Tel (0248) 810415
Access Grade **2**

BETWS-Y-COED

Plas Hall Hotel

Pont-y-Pant, Betws-y-Coed, Gwynedd
LL25 0PJ
Contact: Mr J Williams
Tel (06906) 206
Access Grade **2**

CAERNARFON

Richard Wilson Arts Centre

Plas Baladeulyn, Nantlle, Penygroes,
Caernarfon, Gwynedd LL54 6BW
Tel (0286) 880676
Access Grade **1**

The Stables Hotel

Llanwnda, Caernarfon, Gwynedd
LL54 5SD
Contact: Mr A M Evans
Tel (0286) 830711
Access Grade **3**

COLWYN BAY

Ashmount Hotel

College Avenue, Rhos on Sea,
Colwyn Bay, Clwyd LL28 4NT
Contact: Mr & Mrs Stott
Tel (0492) 45479
Access Grade **2**

Edelweiss Hotel

Off Lawson Road, Colwyn Bay, Clwyd
LL29 8HD
Contact: Mr I Burt
Tel (0492) 532314
Access Grade **2**

Northwood Hotel

Rhos on Sea, Colwyn Bay, Clwyd
LL28 4RS
Contact: MR G Palliser
Tel (0492) 49931
Access Grade **2**

DENBIGH

Bryn Glas Hotel

Trefnant, Denbigh, Clwyd
Contact: M M Tibbetts
Tel (0745) 74868
Access Grade **1**

HALKYN

Travel Lodge

A55, Halkyn, Clwyd CH8 8RF
Contact: The Manager
Tel (0352) 780952
Access Grade **2**

LLANBERIS

Royal Victoria Hotel

Llanberis, Gwynedd LL55 4TY
Contact: Mr G Sutherland
Tel (0286) 870253
Access Grade **2**

LLANDUDNO

Ambassador Hotel

Grand Promenade, Llandudno,
Gwynedd LL30 2NR
Contact: Mr D Williams
Tel (0492) 76886
Access Grade **2**

Bedford Hotel

Craig-y-Don Parade, Llandudno,
Gwynedd LL30 1BN
Tel (0492) 76647
Access Grade **2**

Clarence Hotel

Gloddaeth Street, Llandudno,
Gwynedd LL30 2DD
Contact: Mr & Mrs Bracken
Tel (0492) 860193
Access Grade **2**

Epperstone Hotel

Abbey Road, Llandudno, Gwynedd
LL30 2EE
Contact: Mr & Mrs Drew
Tel (0492) 78746
Access Grade **2**

The Grafton Hotel

13-14 Craig-y-Don Parade, Llandudno,
Gwynedd LL30 1BG
Tel (0492) 76814
Access Grade **2**

Marine Hotel

Vaughan Street, Llandudno, Gwynedd
LL30 1AN
Tel (0492) 77521
Access Grade **2**

Royal Hotel

Church Walks, Llandudno, Gwynedd
LL30 2HW
Contact:
Tel (0492) 76476
Access Grade **2**

West Shore Hotel

West Parade, Llandudno, Gwynedd
LL30 2BB
Contact: Mr A K Billington
Tel (0492) 76833
Access Grade **1**

LLANFAIRFECHAN

Aber Falls Hotel

Aber, Llanfairfechan, Gwynedd
LL33 0LN
Contact Mr & Mrs Harvey
Tel (0248) 680579
Access Grade **2**

NORTH WALES ACCOMMODATION

HOTELS

LLANGEFNI

Tre-Ysgawen Hall

Capel Cqch, Llangefni, Gwynedd
Contact: Mrs P Craighead
Tel (0248) 750750
Access Grade 2

LLANGOLLEN

Bryn Howell Hotel

Llangollen, Clwyd LL20 7UW
Contact: Mr & Mrs Lloyd
Tel (0978) 860331
Access Grade 2

Hand Hotel

Bridge Street, Llangollen, Clwyd
LL30 8PL
Contact: Mr D Evans
Tel (0978) 860303
Access Grade 2

RED WHARF BAY

Bryn Tirion Hotel

Red Wharf Bay, Gwynedd LL75 8RZ
Contact: Mr & Mrs Gilholm
Tel (0248) 852366
Access Grade 2

WREXHAM

Travel Lodge

Wrexham Bypass, Rhostyllen,
Wrexham, Clwyd LL14 4ES
Contact: The Manager
Tel (0978) 365705
Access Grade 2

GUEST HOUSES

BENLLECH

Bryn Meirion Guest House

Amlwch Road, Benllech, Gwynedd
LL74 8SR
Contact: Mrs C A Holland
Tel (0248) 853118
Access Grade 1

COLWYN BAY

Holcombe Hotel

9 Grosvenor Gardens, Colwyn Bay,
Clwyd LL29 7YF
Contact: Mrs E Wellings
Tel (0492) 530423
Access Grade 2

PWLLHELI

Tan-y-Foel

Mynytho, Pwllheli, Gwynedd,
LL53 7RL
Contact: Mrs S Dale
Tel (0758) 740807
Access Grade 2

WREXHAM

Lister House

71 Ruabon Road, Wrexham, Clwyd
LL13 7PL
Contact: The Manager
Tel (0978) 263487
Access Grade 1

SELF-CATERING

BENLLECH

Bryn Tiarrob

51 Lon Conwy, Fferam, Benllech,
Gwynedd
Contact: Mr & Mrs Barratt
Tel (0922) 52687
Access Grade 2

Marbuchan

113 Lon Twrcelyn, Fferam, Benllech,
Gwynedd
Contact: Mr & Mrs Barratt
Tel (0922) 52687
Access Grade 2

CAERNARFON

The Old School

Deiniolen, Caernarfon, Gwynedd
LL55 3HH
Contact: Mrs J Halliday
Tel (0286) 871073
Access Grade 2

COLWYN BAY

Hwylfa Ddafydd Country Holidays

Llysfaen, Colwyn Bay, Clwyd
LL29 8TW
Contact: Mr & Mrs D Jones
Tel (0492) 516965
Access Grade 2

CONWY

Horseshoe Cottage

Old Coach House, Talybont, Conwy,
Gwynedd LL32 8SD
Tel (0492) 69782
Access Grade 2

DENBIGH

Howell's School

Denbigh, Clwyd
Contact: Rob Hastings
Tel (0745) 713425
Access Grade 2

HOLYHEAD

Hen Ysgol Holiday Homes

Rhoscolyn, Holyhead, Gwynedd
Contact: Mr & Mrs Van't Wout
Tel (0407) 741593
Access Grade 1

LLANRWST

Glan-y-Borth Bungalows

Glan-y-Borth, Llanrwst, Gwynedd
LL26 OHB
Contact: Mr W R Sudbury
Tel (0492) 641543
Access Grade 1

MENAI BRIDGE

Llyn-y-Gors

Llandegfan, Menai Bridge, Gwynedd
LL59 5PN
Contact: Janet Thompson
Tel (0248) 713410
Access Grade 2

SELF-CATERING

OSWESTRY

Wood Hill

Llansilin, Oswestry.
Contact: Mrs J Kempson
Tel (081) 806 4609
Access Grade 2

PWLLHELI

Cefn Coed & Ysgubor

Chwilog, Pwllheli, Gwynedd
LL53 6NX
Contact: Mrs M Jones
Tel (0766) 810259
Access Grade 2

RUTHIN

Claremont Coach House

Llanycnan, Ruthin, Clwyd LL15 1HD
Tel (08242) 3324
Access Grade 2

CARAVAN HOLIDAY HOME PARKS, TOURING CARAVAN PARKS AND CAMPING SITES

COLWYN BAY

Bron-y-Wendon Caravan Park

Wern Road, Llanddulas, Colwyn Bay,
Clwyd LL22 8HG
Contact: B Harper
Tel (0492) 512903
Access Grade 2

CONWY

Conwy Touring Park

Bwlch Mawr, Conwy, Gwynedd
LL32 8UX
Contact: Mr D N Euston
Tel (0492) 592856
Access Grade 2

Gorse Hill Caravans

Conwy, Gwynedd LL32 8HJ
Contact: Mrs P Sampson
Tel (0492) 593465
Access Grade 2

CRICCIETH

Tyddyn Cethin Caravan Park

Rhoslan, Criccieth, Gwynedd
LL52 0NF
Contact: Mr Cowlishaw
Tel (0766) 522149
Access Grade 3

PORTHMADOG

Garreg Coch Holiday Caravan Park

Morfa Bychan, Porthmadog, Gwynedd
LL49 9YD
Tel (0766) 512210
Access Grade 2

RHYL

Cwybr Caravan Park

Rhuddlan Road, Rhyl, Clwyd
Contact: G Brookes
Tel (0745) 590748
Access Grade 2

MID WALES ACCOMMODATION

HOTELS

ABERYSTWYTH

Llety Gwyn Hotel

Llanbadarn Fawr, Aberystwyth, Dyfed
SY23 3SR
Contact: Mrs S M Jones
Tel (0970) 3965
Access Grade **2**

BUILTH WELLS

Caer Beris Manor

Builth Wells, Powys LD2 3NP
Contact: Mr P Smith
Tel (0982) 552601
Access Grade **1**

DOLGELLAU

Clifton House Hotel

Smithfield Square, Dolgellau,
Gwynedd LL40 1ES
Contact: Mr R A Dix
Tel (0341) 422554
Access Grade **2**

George III Hotel

Penmaenpool, Dolgellau, Gwynedd
LL40 1YD
Contact: Miss Gail Hall
Tel (0341) 422525
Access Grade **2**

GLYNARTHEN

Penbontbren Farm Hotel

Glynarthen, Llandysul, Dyfed SA44 6PE
Contact: Mrs Humphries
Tel (0239) 810248
Access Grade **2**

LLANDRINDOD WELLS

Corven Hall

Howey, Llandrindod Wells, Powys
LD1 5RE
Contact: Mrs B Prince
Tel (0597) 3368
Access Grade **2**

LLANGAMMARCH WELLS

The Lake Hotel

Llangammarch Wells, Powys LD4 4BS
Contact: Mr J P Mifsud
Tel (05912) 202
Access Grade **2**

TALSARNAU

Hotel Maes-y-Neuadd

Talsarnau, Gwynedd LL47 6YA
Contact: Mrs J Slatter
Tel (0766) 780200
Access Grade **2**

GUEST HOUSES

BALA

Talybont Isa Farm

Rhyduchaf, Bala, Gwynedd LL23 7SD
Contact: Mrs A Skinner
Tel (0678) 520234
Access Grade **2**

BUILTH WELLS

Nant-y-Ddefw Farm

Cwmbach, Builth Wells, Powys
LD2 3RU
Contact: Mr & Mrs Phillips
Tel (0982) 553675
Access Grade **2**

CARDIGAN

The Old Vicarage

Moylegrove, Cardigan, Dyfed
SA43 3BN
Contact: Mr A L Govey
Tel (023986) 231
Access Grade **2**

LAMPETER

Bryn Castell

Llanfair Road, Lampeter, Dyfed
SA48 8JY
Contact: Mrs B Davies
Tel (0570) 422447
Access Grade **2**

MACHYNLLETH

Plas Dyfi

Pennal, Machynlleth, Powys
Contact: Mrs D M Hutchinson
Tel (0654) 75688
Access Grade **3**

TRAWSFYNYDD

Old Mill Farmhouse

Fronoleu Farm, Trawsfynydd,
Gwynedd LL41 4UN
Contact: Mrs R C Bain
Tel (076687) 397
Access Grade **2**

WELSHPOOL

Old Mill House

Llanfair Caereinion, Welshpool,
Powys SY21 0SB
Contact: Mr & Mrs R J Burton
Tel (0938) 810623
Access Grade **2**

SELF-CATERING

CARDIGAN

Gorslwyd Farm

Tan y Groes, Cardigan, Dyfed
SA43 2HZ
Contact: Mr & Mrs Donaldson
Tel (0239) 810593
Access Grade **1**

The Stables

Castell Malgwyn, Llechryd, Cardigan,
Dyfed
Contact: Mrs Watson
Tel (023987) 777
Access Grade **2**

LAMPETER

Cefnbryn Farm

Cwmann, Lampeter, Dyfed SA48 8DX
Contact: Mrs Symons
Tel (0570) 422079
Access Grade **2**

SELF-CATERING

LAMPETER

Gaer Cottages

Cribyn, Lampeter, Dyfed SA48 7LZ
Contact: Mr I W F Sharp
Tel (0570) 470275
Access Grade **1**

LLWYNGWRIL

Pentre Bach

Llwyngwril, Gwynedd LL37 2JU
Contact: Mr & Mrs N D Smyth
Tel (0341) 250294
Access Grade **2**

MACHYNLLETH

Dolau

Maesteg, Darowen, Machynlleth,
Powys
Contact: Mrs S C Pughe
Tel (06502) 598
Access Grade **3**

Dolguog Hall

Machynlleth, Powys SY20 8US
Contact: G J Pritchard
Tel (0654) 2244
Access Grade **3**

NEW QUAY

Tŷ Hen Farm

Llwyndafydd, New Quay, Dyfed
SA44 6BZ
Contact: Mr & Mrs Kelly
Tel (0545) 560346
Access Grade **2**

NEWTOWN

Fir House Farm

Tregynon, Newtown, Powys
Contact: Mr & Mrs P A Jones
Tel (0686) 87217
Access Grade **2**

CARAVAN HOLIDAY HOME PARKS, TOURING CARAVAN PARKS AND CAMPING SITES

ABERYSTWYTH

Glan-y-Mor Leisure Park

Clarach Bay, Aberystwyth, Dyfed
SY23 3DT
Contact: Mr P Bourne
Tel (0970) 828900
Access Grade Caravans **2**
Access Grade Amenities **2**

BALA

Bryn Melyn Leisure Park

Llandderfel, Bala, Gwynedd
LL23 7RA
Contact: A & B Ward
Tel (06783) 212
Access Grade **2**

BORTH

Cambrian Coast Holiday Park

Ynyslas, Borth, Dyfed
Contact: Mr & Mrs Ferguson
Tel (097081) 366
Access Grade **2**

LLANDYSUL

Pilbach Caravan/Camp Park

Bettws Ifan, Rhydlewis, Llandysul,
Dyfed SA44 5RT
Contact: Peter & Stuart Eccleston
Tel (023975) 434
Access Grade **3**

MACHYNLLETH

Warren Parc Caravan Park

Penegoes, Machynlleth, Powys
Contact: Mr I R Warren
Tel (06554) 2054
Access Grade **2**

RHAYADER

Wyeside Caravan/Camp Park

Aberystwyth Road, Rhayader, Powys
Contact: Mr P Humphreys
Tel (0597) 3737
Access Grade **3**

TYWYN

Ynysmaengwyn Caravan Park

Tywyn, Gwynedd
Contact: Tywyn Town Council
Tel (0654) 710684
Access Grade **2**

SOUTH WALES ACCOMMODATION

HOTELS

BRECON

Bishop's Meadow Hotel

Hay Road, Brecon, Powys LD3 9SW
Contact: Mrs D E Parry
Tel (0874) 2051
Access Grade 2

Castle of Brecon Hotel

The Avenue, Brecon, Powys
LD3 9DB
Contact: Mr R Eggins
Tel (0874) 4611
Access Grade 1

BRIDGEND

Travel Lodge

Sarn Park, Bridgend, Mid Glamorgan
Contact: Mrs Shillam
Tel (0656) 659218
Access Grade 2

Travel Lodge

Old Mill, Felindre Road, Pencoed,
Bridgend, Mid Glamorgan CF3 5HO
Contact: The Manager
Tel (0656) 864404
Access Grade 2

CAERPHILLY

Griffin Inn Motel

Rudry, Caerphilly, Mid Glamorgan
Contact: Mr M Evans
Tel (0222) 869735
Access Grade 2

CARDIFF

Copthorne Hotel

Copthorne Way, Culverhouse Cross,
Cardiff, South Glamorgan
Contact: Mr Simon Read
Tel (0222) 599100
Access Grade 2

Holiday Inn

Mill Lane, Cardiff, South Glamorgan
CF1 1EZ
Contact: Mr J Nicholas
Tel (0222) 399944
Access Grade 2

Travel Lodge

Coed-y-Gores, Circle Way East,
Llanedeyrn, Cardiff, South Glamorgan
CF3 7ND
Contact: The Manager
Tel (0222) 549564
Access Grade 2

COWBRIDGE

Jane Hodge Hotel

Nr Cowbridge, South Glamorgan
Tel (0446) 772608
Access Grade 1

CWMBRAN

Parkway Hotel

Cwmbran Drive, Cwmbran, Gwent
NP44 3UW
Contact: Mr J S Woodcock
Tel (0633) 87119
Access Grade 2

FISHGUARD

Fishguard Bay Hotel

Goodwick, Fishguard, Dyfed SA64 0BT
Contact: Mr G J Schell
Tel (0348) 873571
Access Grade 2

LLANDEILO

Plough Inn

Rhosmaen, Llandeilo, Dyfed
SA19 6NP
Contact: Mrs D R Rocca
Tel (0558) 823431
Access Grade 2

LLANELLI

Travel Lodge

Cross Hands, Llanelli,
West Glamorgan SA14 6NW
Contact: The Manager
Tel (0269) 845700
Access Grade 2

MERTHYR TYDFIL

Tregenna Hotel

Park Terrace, Merthyr Tydfil,
Mid Glamorgan CF47 8RF
Contact: Mr M Hurley
Tel (0685) 723627
Access Grade 2

PEMBROKE DOCK

Cleddau Bridge Hotel

Essex Road, Pembroke Dock, Dyfed
SA72 6UT
Contact: Mr Mullen
Tel (0646) 685961
Access Grade 2

PORT TALBOT

Aberafan Beach Hotel

Port Talbot, West Glamorgan
SA12 6QP
Contact: Mr C Meaglia
Tel (0639) 884949
Access Grade 2

SWANSEA

Holiday Inn

Maritime Quarter, Swansea,
West Glamorgan
Contact: Liz Poore
Tel (0792) 642020
Access Grade 1

TENBY

Atlantic Hotel

The Esplanade, Tenby, Dyfed
SA70 7DU
Contact: Mr B James
Tel (0834) 2881
Access Grade 2

Greenhills Hotel

St Florence, Tenby, Dyfed SA70 8NB
Contact: Mrs A Probert
Tel (0834) 871738
Access Grade 2

HOTELS

TENBY

Milton Manor Hotel

Milton, Tenby, Dyfed SA70 8PG
Contact: Mr B Richardson
Tel (0646) 531398
Access Grade 2

USK

Cwrt Bleddyn Hotel

Llangybi, Usk, Gwent NP5 1PG
Contact: Mr J W I Daw
Tel (0633) 49521
Access Grade 3

GUEST HOUSES

CARMARTHEN

Cwmtwrch Farm

Nantgaredig, Carmarthen, Dyfed
SA32 7NY
Contact: Mrs J Wilmott
Tel (0267) 290238
Access Grade 3

OXWICH

Surf Sound

Oxwich, Gower, West Glamorgan
SA3 1LS
Contact: Mr & Mrs Woodburn
Tel (0792) 390822
Access Grade 2

PEMBROKE

Rosedene

Hodgeston, Pembroke, Dyfed SA71
Contact: Mrs E A Fallon
Tel (0646) 672586
Access Grade 1

VISIT A
TOURIST
INFORMATION
CENTRE

PONTARDAWE

Treehaven

Penlan Road, Pontardawe,
West Glamorgan SA8 4RP
Contact: Mrs S Walter
Tel (0792) 830174
Access Grade 2

PORTHCAWL

Oasis

2 South Road, Porthcawl,
Mid Glamorgan CF36 3DG
Contact: Mrs L J Pollard
Tel (0656) 716276
Access Grade 2

ST DAVID'S

Rigsby's

49 Nun Street, St David's, Dyfed
Contact: Mr Armitage
Tel (0437) 720632
Access Grade 2

TENBY

Knightson Lodge

New Hedges, Tenby, Dyfed
SA70 8TL
Contact: J Faulkener
Tel (0834) 2095
Access Grade 2

SELF-CATERING

BRECON

Brynfedwen Farm

(Granary Flat), Trallong Common,
Sennybridge, Brecon, Powys
Contact: Mr M C Adams
Tel (087482) 505
Access Grade 2

BROAD HAVEN

Millmoor Farm Cottages

Broad Haven, Haverfordwest, Dyfed
SA62 3JH
Contact: Mr & Mrs Mock
Tel (0437) 781507
Access Grade 2

CARMARTHEN

Pantgwyn Farm

Whitemill, Carmarthen, Dyfed
SA32 7ES
Contact: Mr & Mrs T E Giles
Tel (0267) 5859
Access Grade 2

CHEPSTOW

Cwrt-y-Gaer

Wolvesnewton, Chepstow, Gwent
NP6 6PR
Contact: Mr & Mrs J Llewellyn
Tel (02915) 700
Access Grade 1

HAVERFORDWEST

Rocksdrift Apartments

Broad Haven, Haverfordwest, Dyfed
SA62 3ED
Contact: E & H Mock
Tel (0437) 781507
Access Grade 2

Rosemoor Country Cottages

Walwyn's Castle, Haverfordwest,
Dyfed SA62 3ED
Contact: Mrs B Lloyd
Tel (0437) 781326
Access Grade 2

KILGETTY

Hanbury Lodge

Jeffreyston, Kilgetty, Dyfed SA68 0RH
Contact: Mr & Mrs Eardley
Tel (0834) 811212
Access Grade 2

MANORBIER

Landway Farm

Manorbier, Dyfed SA70 7SH
Contact: S Thomas
Tel (0834) 871580
Access Grade 2

SELF-CATERING

PEMBROKE

Stackpole Centre

Home Farm, Stackpole, Pembroke, Dyfed
Contact: The Stackpole Trust
Tel (0646) 81425
Access Grade **2**

PORTHCAWL

Oasis

2 South Road, Porthcawl,
Mid Glamorgan CF36 3DG
Contact: Mrs L J Pollard
Tel (0656) 716276
Access Grade **2**

PORT TALBOT

Ty'n y Caeau Chalets

Margam Village, Port Talbot,
West Glamorgan
Contact: Mr & Mrs G F Gaen
Tel (0639) 883897
Access Grade **2**

TENBY

Knightson Lodge Flats

New Hedges, Tenby, Dyfed
SA70 8TL
Contact: J Faulkner
Tel (0834) 2095
Access Grade **2**

CARAVAN HOLIDAY HOME PARKS, TOURING CARAVAN PARKS AND CAMPING SITES

BRECON

Brynich Caravan Park

Brecon, Powys
Contact: C R & A M Jones
Tel (0874) 3325
Access Grade **2**

BRIDGEND

Kenfig Pool Caravan Park

Ton Kenfig, Bridgend,
Mid Glamorgan CF33 4PT
Contact: Mr Theodore
Tel (0656) 712572
Access Grade **3**

BURRY PORT

Shoreline Caravan/ Chalet Park

Burry Port, Dyfed SA16 0HD
Contact: The Director
Tel (05546) 2657
Access Grade **2**

CARDIFF

Pontcanna Caravan Park

Pontcanna Fields, Cardiff,
South Glamorgan CF1 9JJ
Contact: The Warden
Tel (0222) 398362
Access Grade **2**

LLANRHIDIAN

Llanrhidian Caravan Park

Llanrhidian, Gower, West Glamorgan
SA1 1EU
Contact: Mr Theodore
Tel (0792) 391083
Access Grade **2**

PORTHCAWL

Trecco Bay Leisure Park

Porthcawl, Mid Glamorgan
CF36 5NG
Contact: Mr Theodore
Tel (0656) 712103
Access Grade **2**

REYNOLDSTON

Llanddewi

Reynoldston, Gower, West Glamorgan
SA3 1AU
Contact: Mr Theodore
Tel (044122) 330
Access Grade **2**

SAUNDERSFOOT

Saundersfoot Bay Leisure Park

Saundersfoot, Dyfed SA69 9DG
Contact: Mr J Shuttleworth
Tel (0834) 812284
Access Grade Caravans **2**
Access Grade Amenities **2**

ACCOMMODATION

YOUTH HOSTELS/ ACTIVITY CENTRES

NORTH WALES

CAERNARFON

Youth Hostel

Pen y Pass, Nantgwynant, Caernarfon,
Gwynedd LL55 4NY
Contact: Mr & Mrs Lloyd
Tel (0286) 870428
Access Grade 2

MID WALES

LLANYBYDDER

Blaenwern Farm Complex

Llanybydder, Dyfed SA40 9RB
Contact: Mr & Mrs Lamport
Tel (0570) 480078
Access Grade 2

SOUTH WALES

ABERCRAF

Cefn Yr Erw Study Centre

Caehopkin Road, Abercraf,
West Glamorgan
Tel (0639) 730276
Access Grade 2

HAVERFORDWEST

The Youth Hostel

Broad Haven, Haverfordwest, Dyfed
Contact: Mr & Mrs Garner
Tel (0437) 781688
Access Grade 1

TONYPANDY

The Youth Hostel

Glyncorner, Llwynypia, Rhondda,
Mid Glamorgan
Tel (0443) 430859
Access Grade 2

Places to go; Things to do

Wales's beautiful countryside and its wealth of ancient buildings are two of its main attractions. Disabled visitors needn't feel discouraged, for there is a surprising range of accessible and interesting places to visit in Wales. This is thanks to the increasing number of national heritage bodies, national parks and local authorities who now acknowledge that access for disabled people is an issue that they should be addressing. While it is difficult to argue that all the attractions of Wales are accessible, things are gradually improving. Whether you enjoy the countryside, cultural activities, sports or less energetic pleasures, you should find something of interest wherever you are in Wales.

General Information

Information on accessible facilities can be obtained from several conservation and tourist bodies in Wales. These include:

●**Brecon Beacons National Park Office**
7 Glamorgan Street, Brecon, Powys LD3 7DP
Tel (0874) 4437

●**CADW: Welsh Historic Monuments**
Brunel House, 2 Fitzalan Road, Cardiff,
South Glamorgan CF2 1UY
Contact: Liz Peel
Tel (0222) 465511

●**Glamorgan Heritage Coast Centre**
Dunraven Park, Southerndown, Mid Glamorgan
Tel (0656) 880157

●**National Trust**
North Wales Regional Office
Trinity Square, Llandudno, Gwynedd LL30 2DE
Tel (0492) 860123

●**National Trust**
South Wales Regional Office
King's Head, Bridge Street, Llandeilo, Dyfed
SA18 3NL
Tel (0558) 822800

●**Pembrokeshire Coast National Park Office**
County Offices, Haverfordwest, Dyfed
Tel (0437) 764591

●**Royal Society for the Protection of Birds**
The Lodge, Sandy, Bedfordshire
Tel (0767) 680551

●**Snowdonia National Park Office**
Penrhyndeudraeth, Gwynedd
Tel (0766) 770274

CLWYD

BODELWYDDAN

Bodelwyddan Castle
Bodelwyddan

Limited Access

Tel (0745) 584060

Felin-y-Gors Trout Farm & Fisheries
Bodelwyddan

Easy access for wheelchair-bound anglers.

Tel (0745) 584044

CAERGWRLE

Waun-y-Llyn Country Park
Nr Caergwrle (A541)

Tel (035285) 586

COLWYN BAY

Welsh Mountain Zoo
Colwyn Bay

Tel (0492) 532938

Dinosaur World
Eirias Park, Colwyn Bay

Accessible WC to be built in 1991.

Tel (0492) 518111

CERRIGYDRUDION

Bod Petrual Picnic Site
In Clocaenog Forest on B5105
6 miles, nr Cerrigydrudion.

Accessible WC

Llyn Brenig Reservoir
Nr Cerrigydrudion

Picnic Sites and accessible WC. Ramped fishing platforms for disabled anglers.

Tel (049082) 463

DENBIGH

Denbigh Castle (CADW)
Denbigh.

Ticket office and exhibition accessible to wheelchair users. Most of castle can be viewed with a helper.

Denbigh Friary (CADW)
Denbigh

Access through a gate.

Leicester's Church (CADW)
Denbigh

Access possible via a gate.

St Hilary's Chapel (CADW)
Denbigh

Mostly viewed from exterior.

Yur Hen Felin Museum Crafts Shop
Pentre, Llanrhaedr, Denbigh

Tel (074578) 239

DERWEN

Derwen Churchyard Cross (CADW)
Derwen

Two steps into churchyard.

FLINT

Flint Castle (CADW)

Ground level access for wheelchair users with helper.

GLYNCEIRIOG

Chwarel Wynne Slate Mine
Glynceiriog

Tel (069172) 343

HOLYWELL

Basingwerk Abbey (CADW)
Holywell

Most of the Abbey is suitable for wheelchairs or can be viewed from the perimeter.

Greenfield Valley Heritage/Abbey Farm Museum
Holywell

Tel (0352) 714127

LLANGOLLEN

European Centre for Folk Studies
Parade Street, Llangollen

Tel (0978) 861292

Llangollen Canal & Barges
Trefor Basin, Llangollen

(Tel) 0978 860702

Llangollen Craft Centre
Llangollen

Tel (0978) 861887

Llangollen Motor Museum
Pentrefelin, Llangollen

Tel (0978) 860324

Llangollen Steam Railway
Llangollen

Tel (0978) 860951

Llantysilio Picnic Site
Llangollen. On B5103, 200 yards north of A5

Accessible WC.

Vale of Llangollen Canal Boat Trust
East Street, Llangollen

Boat Hire

Tel (0978) 861450

Valle Crucis Abbey (CADW)
Nr Llangollen

Suitable for wheelchair users with helper.

MOLD

Daniel Owen Gallery
Earl Road, Mold

Tel (0352) 4791

Loggerheads Country Park
Mold

Accessible WC.

Tel (035285) 586

Oriel Gallery
Theatr Clwyd, Civic Centre, Mold

Tel (0352) 56331

CLWYD

MOLD

Tri Thy Craft Centre
Coed Talon, nr Mold
Tel (0352) 771359

MOSTYN

Abakhan Rugs Mill Shop
Llanerch-y-Mor, Coast Road, Mostyn
Ground floor only.
Tel (0745) 560312

PRESTATYN

Nova Centre
Central Beach, Prestatyn
Tel (07456) 88021

RHUDDLAN

Rhuddlan Castle (CADW)
Rhuddlan
*Suitable for wheelchair users with helper.
Ground level access only.*

RHYL

Knights Caverns
38 - 41 West Parade, Rhyl
Tel (0745) 338562

Rhyl Library, Museum and Arts Centre
Church Street, Rhyl
Tel (0745) 353814

Rhyl Sun Centre
Promenade, Rhyl
Tel (0745) 344433

RUTHIN

Moel Famau Country Park
Ruthin, (A494)
Accessible WC
Tel (035285) 586

Ruthin Craft Centre
Ruthin
Accessible WC
Tel (08242) 4774

ST ASAPH

St Asaph Cathedral
St Asaph
Special entrance for wheelchairs.

WREXHAM

Bersham Industrial Heritage Centre
Wrexham
Tel (0978) 261529

Clywedog Valley Heritage Park
Felin Puleston, nr Wrexham
Easy access to centre, wheelchair paths through conservation area.
Tel (0978) 264470

Erddig (National Trust)
Nr Wrexham LL13 0YT
Access limited to ground floor, outbuildings and garden. Visitors wishing to bring their own wheelchairs are asked to phone in advance.
Tel (0978) 355314

Ty Mawr Country Park
Ruabon, nr Wrexham
Tel (0978) 822780

Wrexham Arts Centre
Rhosddu Road, Wrexham
Tel (0978) 2351

DYFED

ABERYSTWYTH

**Aberystwyth Arts Centre Gallery,
Catherine Lewis Gallery,
Ceramic Gallery,
University College of Wales**
Penglais Hill, Aberystwyth
Tel (0970) 623339

Ceredigion Museum
13 Eastgate, Aberystwyth
Tel (0970) 617911

Rheidol Power Station
Cwm Rheidol, nr Aberystwyth
Mostly accessible with help.
Tel (0970) 84667

BORTH

Borth Livestock Centre Animalarium
Ynys Fergi, Borth SY24 5NA
Entrance, cafe, shop and WC (not adapted) accessed via a ramp.
Tel (0970) 871224

CARDIGAN

Blaenporth Gallery, Old School Studio
Blaenporth, Cardigan
Tel (0239) 810482

CARMARTHEN

Carmarthen Museum
Abergwili
Tel (0267) 231691

Pontarffinant Picnic Site
Overlooking River Twyi on B3400,
1 mile east of junction with B4310,
nr Carmarthen
Accessible WC.

DEVIL'S BRIDGE

Ystwyth Forest Walk Nature Reserve
Nr Devil's Bridge, (B4574 from A4120)
Accessible WC.
Tel (09743) 404

HAVERFORDWEST

Haverfordwest Library Gallery
Dew Street, Haverfordwest
Tel (0437) 2070. Tel (0437) 4920

PLACES TO GO; THINGS TO DO

Llys-y-Fran Country Park,
Nr Haverfordwest
Tel (0437) 532694
Tel (0437) 532273

HAVERFORDWEST

Scolton Manor Country Park & Museum
Nr Spittal
Accessible WC.
Tel (0437) 82457

KIDWELLY

Kidwelly Castle (CADW)
Kidwelly
Ground level access for wheelchair users with helper.

Kidwelly Industrial Museum
Kidwelly
Tel (0554) 891078

LLANDEILO

Gelli Aur Country Park
Nr Llandeilo
Tel (05584) 885

LLANELLI

Lliedi Reservoir
Nr Llanelli
Ramped fishing platform. Woodland trail suitable for visually handicapped visitors.
Tel (0874) 3181

Llanelli Library Exhibition Gallery
Vaughn Street, Llanelli
Tel (0554) 3538

LLANDYSUL

Maesllyn Woollen Mill Museum
Maesllyn, nr Llandysul
Tel (0239) 75251

Museum of the Welsh Woollen Industry
Dre-Fach Felindre, nr Llandysul
SA44 5UP
Level ground floor access to woollen mill and craft workshops.
Accessible WC
Tel (0559) 370929

MACHYNLLETH

Dyfi Forest, Tan-y-Coed & Foel Friog Picnic Sites
Nr Machynlleth, (A487)
Accessible WC.
Tel (09743) 404

Ynys Hir Reserve (RSPB)
Eglwys Fach, nr Machynlleth
SY20 8TA
Woodlands and estuary walks suitable for people in wheelchairs with strong pusher, or car access by arrangement. One observation hide and WC accessible.
Tel (0654) 781265

NARBERTH

Oakwood Park
Canaston Bridge, nr Narberth
Adventure park, reduced rates for disabled visitors.
Tel (0834) 891376

Transit Picnic Site
1½ miles north of Narberth at junction of A40 and A478
Accessible WC.

NEWCASTLE EMLYN

Felin Geri Mill
Felin Geri, Cwm-Cou,
nr Newcastle Emlyn SA38 9PA
Mostly accessible to wheelchairs with assistance.
Tel (0239) 710810

PEMBREY

Pembrey Country Park
Waun Sidan, Pembrey
Disabled route; accessible WC in Visitor Centre.
Tel (05546) 3913

PEMBROKE

Stackpole (National Trust)
Nr Pembroke
Walk suitable for wheelchair users, accessible WC.

Stackpole Quarry Project (National Trust)
Outdoor activities; clifftop walk

PEMBROKESHIRE

Pembrokeshire National Park Coast Path
Pembrokeshire
For details of 16 walks suitable for people with disabilities please contact the National Park Office, Haverfordwest (see general information at start of this section).

ST DAVID'S

Oceanarium
New Street, St David's SA62 6SS
Level access to ground floor but no lift to first floor, wheelchair users and their companions admitted free.
Tel (0437) 720453

Thousand Islands Expeditions
Cross Square, St David's SA62 6SL
Tours of Pembrokeshire's offshore islands.
Tel (0437) 721686

TENBY

Manor House Wildlife & Leisure Park
St Florence, nr Tenby
Tel (0646) 651201

MID GLAMORGAN

ABERDARE

Dare Valley Country Park
Nr Aberdare (off A4059)
Accessible WC.
Tel (0685) 874672

BARGOED

Parc Cwm Darran Country Park
Nr Bargoed (A469)
Accessible WC.
Tel (0443) 875557

BRIDGEND

Ewenny Priory (CADW)
Ewenny, nr Bridgend
Most of site can be viewed with helper.

Kenfig Pool Nature Reserve
Nr Pyle, B4281 from M4 exit 37
Accessible WC.
Tel (0222) 820748

Park Pond Nature Reserve
Glamorgan Nature Centre, Fountain Road, Tondu, Bridgend
Boardwalk, bird hide and accessible WC.
Tel (0656) 724100

CAERPHILLY

Caerphilly Castle (CADW)
Wheelchair access at ground level with helper.

LLANTRISANT

Model House Craft and Design Centre
Bullring, Llantrisant CF7 8EB
Tel (0443) 237758

MERTHYR TYDFIL

Cyfartha Castle Museum
Cyfartha Park, Merthyr Tydfil
Tel (0685) 723201

Cwm Taff Reservoir
A470 Brecon-Merthyr Road
Accessible WC.
Tel (087487) 260

Llwyn-Onn Reservoir
Between Brecon and Merthyr
Tel (0685) 723060

NELSON

Llancaiach Fawr
Nelson
Visitor Centre and Museum. Wheelchair access to ground floor of house, grounds and all visitor centre facilities. Accessible WC and lifts.
Tel (0443) 815588

OGMORE

Ogmore Castle (CADW)
Wheelchair access at ground level with helper.

PONTYPRIDD

Pontypridd Historical & Cultural Centre
Bridge Street, Pontypridd
Lift, accessible WC.
Tel (0443) 402077

PORTHCAWL

Porthcawl Museum
Old Police Station, John Street
Tel (0656) 712211

SOUTHERNDOWN

Dunraven Park/Glamorgan Heritage Coast Park
Nr Southerndown (B4181)
Accessible WC.
Tel (0656) 880157

TREHAFOD

Rhondda Heritage Park
Coed Cae Road, Trehafod, Rhondda
Ramp to winding house, lift to first floor of visitor centre, accessible WC.
Tel (0443) 682036

SOUTH GLAMORGAN

BARRY

Porthkerry Country Park
Nr Barry
Tel (0446) 733589

S.S. Waverley
Gwalia Buildings, Barry Docks, Barry
Sea cruises.
Accessible WC, help available on request.
Tel (0446) 720656

Welsh Hawking Centre
Weycock Road, Barry
Assistance and facilities available on request.
Tel (0446) 734687

CARDIFF

Cardiff Castle
Duke Street, Kingsway, Cardiff
Access to grounds only.
Tel (0222) 822083

Cardiff City Farm
Rear of Sloper Road, Cardiff
Tel (0222) 384360

Chapter Arts Centre
Market Road, Canton, Cardiff
Tel (0222) 396061/236244/399666

Dyffryn Gardens
St Nicholas, Cardiff
Wheelchair available, easy access around grounds.
Tel (0222) 593328

PLACES TO GO; THINGS TO DO

Fforest Farm Conservation Centre
Nr Whitchurch Village (exit 30 off M4)
Accessible WC.
Tel (0222) 626660

Llanishen & Lisvane Reservoirs
Nr Cardiff (off B4562)
Accessible WC.
Tel (0874) 3181

National Museum of Wales
Cathays Park, Cardiff
Entrance via Porter's lodge. Accessible WC. Wheelchairs available.
Tel (0222) 397951

Parc Cefn Onn
Nr Cardiff (off A469)
Accessible WC.
Tel (0222) 751235

Roath Park
Cardiff
Accessible WC.
Tel (0222) 751235

Sherman Theatre Gallery
University College, Senghenydd Road, Cardiff
Tel (0222) 396844

Techniquest
72 Bute Street, Pierhead, Cardiff
Tel (0222) 460211

Welsh Folk Museum
St Fagans, Cardiff
Accessible WC. Access to restaurant, museum and grounds; limited access to exhibits and main house.
Tel (0222) 569441

Welsh Industrial & Maritime Museum
Bute Street, Cardiff
Tel (0222) 481919

LLANTWIT MAJOR

St Donat's Art Centre
St Donat's Castle, Llantwit Major
Telephone beforehand, help available
Tel (0446) 794848

PENARTH

Cosmeston Lakes Country Park
Nr Penarth (via B4267)
Accessible WC.
Tel (0222) 701678

PENDOYLAN

Llanerch Vineyard
Hensol, Pendoylan, Vale of Glamorgan CF7 8JU
Facilities provided for visitors with disabilities - please telephone to arrange parking.
Tel (0443) 225877

Welsh Folk Museum,
St Fagans.

WEST GLAMORGAN

LLANRHIDIAN

Weobley Castle (CADW)
Nr Llanrhidian, Gower
Limited access. Good views.

NEATH

Aberdulais Falls (National Trust)
Aberdulais, Neath
Information centre and part of site accessible.
Tel (0639) 636674

Cefn Coed Colliery Museum
Blaenant Colliery, Crynant, nr Neath
Tel (0639) 750556

Neath Abbey (CADW)
Ground floor accessible with helper.

PORT EYNON

Port Eynon Village
Gower
Accessible WC.
Tel (0792) 50821

PORT TALBOT

Afan Argoed Country Park
Nr Port Talbot
Accessible WC. Electric wheelchair loan.
Tel (0639) 850564

Margam Country Park
Nr Port Talbot
Accessible WC, visitor centre, pony trekking, orangery, farm trail, etc.
Tel (0639) 871131

Margam Stones Museum (CADW)
Adjacent to Margam Country Park
Site level but space restricted.

Welsh Miner's Museum
Afan Argoed Country Park,
nr Port Talbot
Accessible WC. Admission free for disabled visitors and their companions.
Tel (0639) 850564

RHOSILI

Rhosili Nature Reserve (National Trust)
Coastguard Cottages, Rhosili, Gower
SA3 1PR
Exhibition and shop accessible.
Tel (0792) 390707

SWANSEA

Glynn Vivian Art Gallery
Alexandra Road, Swansea
Ground floor accessible; remainder accessible by prior arrangement.
Tel (0792) 651738

Plantasia Tropical Hothouse
North Dock, Swansea
Tel (0792) 474555

Swansea Maritime & Industrial Museum
Museum Square, Maritime Quarter,
Swansea
Tel (0792) 650351

GWENT

BLAENAFON

Big Pit Mining Museum
Blaenafon
Prior arrangement essential.
Tel (0495) 790311

CAERLEON

Caerleon Roman Baths & Amphitheatre (CADW)
All of baths site accessible, most of amphitheatre can be viewed.

Legionary Museum (National Museum of Wales)
High Street, Caerleon
Tel (0633) 423134

CALDICOT

Caldicot Castle & Country Park
Caldicot (off A48)
Accessible WC.
Tel (0291) 420241

CHEPSTOW

Chepstow Castle (CADW)
Accessible at ground level with helper.

CWMBRAN

Greenmeadow Community Farm
Cwmbran
Tel (06333) 62202

Llantarnam Grange Arts Centre
Cwmbran
Tel (06333) 3321

LLANTILIO CROSSENNY

White Castle (CADW)
Llantilio Crossenny, nr Abergavenny
Ground floor access for wheelchair users with helper.

MONMOUTH

Grosmont Castle (CADW)
North of Monmouth
Most of site can be viewed with a helper.

The Kymin (National Trust)
Nr Monmouth
Wheelchair accessible paths through wooded area.

Monmouth Museum
Priory Street, Monmouth
Tel (0600) 713519

PLACES TO GO; THINGS TO DO

NEWPORT

Fourteen Locks Canal Picnic Site
Rogerstone, Newport
Tel (0633) 894802 Summer
Tel (0633) 832787 Winter

Newport Museum & Art Gallery
John Frost Square, Newport
Tel (0633) 840064

Tredegar House & Park
Newport
Accessible WC.
Tel (0633) 815880

OAKDALE

Pen-y-Fan Pond Country Park
Oakdale
Tel (0495) 214753

PONTYPOOL

Llandegfedd Reservoir
Pontypool
Tel (0495) 755122

Valley Inheritance
Park Buildings, Pontypool
Tel (0495) 752043

RAGLAN

Raglan Castle (CADW)
Limited ground floor access.

TINTERN

Old Station
Tintern
Tel (0633) 804802 Summer
Tel (0633) 832787 Winter

Tintern Abbey (CADW)
Accessible for wheelchair users with helper.

Tintern Forest
Nr Tintern (A466)
Accessible WC.
Tel (0633) 400205

TREDEGAR

Bryn Bach Park
Tredegar
Tel (0495) 711816

USK

Gwent Rural Life Museum
New Market Street, Usk
Tel (02913) 3777

Whitehall Picnic Area
Nr Usk, both sides A449 - 3 miles
north-east of M4 junction 24
Accessible WC.

GWYNEDD

BANGOR

Bangor Art Gallery
Ffordd Gwynedd, Bangor
Tel (0248) 53368

David Windsor Gallery
201 High Street, Bangor
Tel (0248) 4639

Museum of Welsh Antiquities
Ffordd Gwynedd, Bangor
Tel (0248) 4639

Penrhyn Castle (National Trust)
Nr Bangor
Ground floor of house, tearoom and parts of garden and park accessible. Accessible WC.
Tel (0248) 353084

BEAUMARIS

Beaumaris Gaol & Courthouse
Beaumaris, Anglesey
Access to gaol only.
Tel (0248) 750262

Museum of Childhood
Beaumaris, Anglesey
Ground floor only.
Tel (0248) 810448

Time Tunnel
The Green, Beaumaris, Anglesey
Tel (0248) 810072

BETHESDA

Bryn Derwen Centre
Bethesda
Tel (028628) 602112

BETWS-Y-COED

Conwy Valley Railway Museum
Betws-y-Coed
Accessible WC.
Tel (0690) 710568

Y Stablau Visitor Centre (Snowdonia National Park)
Exhibition and audio-visual theatre accessible.

BLAENAU FFESTINIOG

Ffestiniog Power Station
Tan-y-Grisiau, Blaenau Ffestiniog
Tel (0766) 830310

Gloddfa Ganol Mountain Centre
Blaenau Festiniog
Tel (0766) 830664

Llechwedd Slate Caverns
Blaenau Festiniog
Shops and snack bar accessible, prior arrangement essential.
Tel (0766) 830306

BRYNSIENCYN

Anglesey Sea Zoo
Brynsiencyn, Anglesey
Tel (0248) 40041

VISIT A TOURIST INFORMATION CENTRE

PLACES TO GO; THINGS TO DO

CAERNARFON

Plas Menai National Watersports Centre
Llanfairisgaer, nr Caernarfon
Tel (0286) 670964

Segontium Roman Fort & Museum
Beddgelert Road, Caernarfon
Tel (0286) 5625

Seiont II Maritime Museum
Victoria Dock, Caernarfon
Tel: (0286) 4693

CLYNNOG FAWR

Museum of Welsh Country Life
Felin Faesog, Tai'r Lon, Clynnog Fawr
Ground level only.
Tel (0286) 86311

CONWY

Bodnant Garden (National Trust)
Nr Conwy
Tel (0492) 67460

Conwy Butterfly House
Bodlondeb Park, Conwy
Tel (0492) 593149

Conwy Castle (CADW)
Conwy
Entrance via shop. Exhibition accessible to wheelchairs, steep path to castle.

CORRIS

Corris Railway Museum
Station Yard, Corris
Tel (0654) 73624

Tan-y-Coed Picnic Site
Beside A487, 3½ miles north of Machynlleth
Accessible WC.

DINAS DINLLE

Caernarfon Air World
Caernarfon Airport, Dinas Dinlle
Tel (0286) 830800

DOLGELLAU

Coed y Brenin Visitor Centre
Off A470 north of Dolgellau, nr Ganllwyd
Accessible WC.
Tel (0341) 422289

Ganllwyd (National Trust)
Nr Dolgellau
Accessible riverside picnic area, wheelchair access round lake.

Mawddach Valley (RSPB)
Nr Dolgellau
Accessible path and WC (summer only).

Penmaenpool Wildlife Centre (RSPB)
On A493 2 miles west of Dolgellau
Accessible WC.

GAERWEN

Herb Garden Nursery
Pentre Berw, Gaerwen, Anglesey
Tel (0248) 421064

HOLYHEAD

Holyhead Maritime Museum
Rhos y Gaer Avenue, Holyhead, Anglesey
Tel (0407) 2816

Llyn Alaw Reservoir
Llantrisant, Holyhead, Anglesey
Exhibition and picnic areas accessible, adapted toilets. Angling for people with disabilities at reduced rates.
Tel (0407) 730762

LLANBERIS

Power of Wales Museum of the North
Llanberis
Tel (0286) 870636

Quarry Hospital Visitor Centre
Padarn Country Park, Llanberis
Tel (0286) 870892

Welsh Slate Museum
Llanberis
Tel (0286) 870630

LLANDUDNO

Great Orme Cable Car
Llandudno
Tel (0492) 77205

Llandudno Museum
17-19 Gloddaeth Street, Llandudno
Tel (0492) 76517

Llandudno Pier
Off north end of Llandudno Promenade

Rapallo House Museum & Art Gallery
Fferm Bach Road, Craig-y-Don, Llandudno
Tel (0492) 76517

St Tudno's Church
Great Orme, Llandudno

LLANFAIR P G

Plas Newydd (National Trust)
Llanfair P G, Anglesey LL61 6EQ
Access ramps available to ground floor. Accessible WC. Shop, tearoom and garden accessible.
Tel (0248) 714795

LLANGEFNI

Stone Science
Bryn Eglwys, Llanddyfnan, nr Llangefni, Anglesey
Tel (0248) 70310

LLANRUG

Bryn Bras Castle
Llanrug, nr Caernarfon
Wheelchair access to gardens via second entrance.
Tel (0286) 870210

PLACES TO GO; THINGS TO DO

LLANRWST

Gwydir Uchaf Chapel (CADW)
Llanrwst

Accessible to wheelchair users with helper.

LLANYSTUMDWY

Lloyd George Memorial Museum
Llanystumdwy, nr Criccieth
Tel (0766) 522171

LLŶN PENINSULA

Llŷn Peninsula

*Accessible viewpoints with car parking.
Accessible WC at Plas-yn-Rhiw,
Aberdaron (National Trust), but limited
access to house and garden.*

MAENTWROG

Coed Cae Vali (National Trust)
Nr Maentwrog

Accessible picnic site.

MENAI BRIDGE

Tegfryn Art Gallery
Cadnant Road, High Street,
Menai Bridge, Anglesey
Tel (0248) 712437

NEWBOROUGH

Newborough Forest
Nr Newborough Village, Anglesey
Accessible WC.
Tel (0341) 422289

PORTHMADOG

Ffestiniog Railway
Harbour Station, Porthmadog
Tel (0766) 2384

Porthmadog Maritime Museum
Greaves Wharf, Porthmadog
Tel (0766) 513736

Portmeirion Italianate Village
Nr Porthmadog
Tel (0766) 770228

PWLLHELI

Butlins Starcoast World
Tel: (0758) 612112

SNOWDONIA NATIONAL PARK

Morfa Mawddach, Snowdonia
Accessible picnic site, walk and WC.

TYWYN

Narrow-Gauge Railway Museum
Wharf Station, Tywyn
Tel (0654) 710472

POWYS

BRECON

Brecknock Museum
Captain's Walk, Brecon
Tel (0874) 4121

Mountain Centre (Brecon Beacons National Park)
Libanus, nr Brecon
*Wheelchair access to all parts of building,
accessible WC.*
Tel (0874) 3366

South Wales Borderers Regimental Museum
The Watton, Brecon
Tel (0874) 3111 ext 2310

Talybont Reservoir
Off A40/B4558 from Brecon
*Visitor information point in Aber
Clydach.*
Tel (0874) 87307

CRICKHOWELL

Tretower Court (CADW)
Nr Crickhowell
*Ground floor access only, ramps in main
rooms.*

BUILTH WELLS

Erwood Station Craft Centre
6 miles south of Builth Wells on B4567
Tel (0982) 553674

LLANDRINDOD WELLS

Mid Wales Craft Gallery
Newbridge on Wye, nr Llandrindod
Wells LD1 6LY
Tel (059789) 364

LLANFAIR CAEREINION

Welshpool & Llanfair Light Railway
The Station, Llanfair Caereinion
Tel (0938) 810441

LLANIDLOES

Llyn Clywedog Reservoir
Nr Llanidloes (A470)
Accessible WC.
Tel (0743) 231666

LLANWDDYN

Lake Vyrnwy Reserve (RSPB)
Nr Llanwddyn (B4393)
*Nature Trail, bird hide, information
centre and WC all accessible.*
Tel (0691) 73278

MACHYNLLETH

Centre for Alternative Technology
Nr Machynlleth
Tel (0654) 702400

Felin Crewi
Penegoes, nr Machynlleth
*Working watermill, riverside walks and
cafe all accessible.*
Tel (0654) 703113

PLACES TO GO; THINGS TO DO

MONTGOMERY

Montgomery Castle (CADW)
Most of castle can be viewed.

NEWTOWN

Davies Memorial Gallery
Tel (0686) 26220

RHAYADER

Elan Valley Visitor Centre
Elan Village, nr Rhayader
Tel (0597) 810880

TALGARTH

Howell Harris Museum
Trefeca, nr Talgarth
Tel (0874) 711423

Pwll-y-Wrach Nature Reserve (Brecknock Wildlife Trust)
Talgarth, nr Brecon
Wheelchair accessible path.
Tel (0874) 5708

WELSHPOOL

Montgomery Canal Boat Hire
Greenacre, Salop Road, Welshpool
Tel (0938) 553215

Powis Castle
Nr Welshpool
Access to part of grounds only.
Tel (0938) 4336

Powysland Museum
Salop Road, Welshpool
Tel (0938) 554759

Severn Farm Pond Reserve (Montgomery Wildlife Trust)
Welshpool
Tel (0686) 624751

Beaches

Sandy beaches inevitably present problems for anybody with mobility difficulties, especially for wheelchair users. But access to beaches, particularly those with a larger tidal range which packs the sand harder, is not impossible and many beaches have slipways for boat trailers which can make access easier. Less adventurous travellers can make use of the promenades, redolent of a more elegant era, that are still a feature of many Welsh resorts.

CLWYD

- *Colwyn Bay:* Promenade and pier.
- *Old Colwyn:* Promenade.
- *Pensarn:* Promenade.
- *Prestatyn:* Promenade and Nova Centre.
- *Rhyl:* Promenade and Sun Centre.

DYFED

- *Aber Eiddi Bay:* Large car park, pebbles, rock and 'black sand' at low tide.
- *Amroth:* Large car park, shops, pubs, sandy beach with pebble bank.
- *Broad Haven:* Large sandy beach, car parks, boat slipways give access to hard sand at low tide.
- *Freshwater East:* Large sandy beach backed by sand dunes, southern end rocks and shingle. Several parking areas, dangerous for bathing.
- *Gelliswick Bay:* Shingle and silt, car parking along sea front and picnic site.
- *Little Haven:* Small sandy beach, pebbles above high tide line, boat ramp, car park, shops, telephone.
- *Manorbier:* Sandy with pebble bank, car park near castle.
- *Newport Sands:* Large sandy beach backed by sand dunes, car park.
- *Poppit Sands:* Large sandy beach backed by dunes, car park, telephone. Not safe for bathing.
- *Pwll Gwaelod:* Small sandy beach with some parking and picnic site.
- *Saundersfoot:* Large sandy beach, large car park, shops, telephone.
- *Tenby:* Large sandy beaches with good access to south beach, castle and harbour beaches. Close to town
- *Whitesands Bay/Porth Mawr:* Large sandy beach, large car park, cafe, shop, telephone. Dangerous currents off parts of beach.

MID GLAMORGAN

- *Porthcawl:*
- *Newton:* Car park and slipway.
- *Sandy Bay:* Slipway access at west end of funfair promenade.

- *Esplanade:* Slipway access to tarmac 'beach' and split-level promenade.
- *Rest Bay:* Car park and access to common overlooking beach.

SOUTH GLAMORGAN

- *Col-Huw Beach, Llantwit Major:* Follow signs for beach road. Access to car park and cafe but not the beach.
- *Fontygary:* Off B4265 near Cardiff-Wales Airport. Follow signs for Fontygary Bay Caravan Park. Clifftop accessible with help. Accessible WC.
- *The Knap:* Follow signs for Barry Island, then for The Knap. Wide path runs the length of the beach. Accessible WC.
- *Penarth:* Flat, wide esplanade with seating and easy access to pier. Accesible WC.
- *Porthkerry Beach:* Adjoining Porthkerry Country Park, Barry. Path from car park to beach accessible, but not the beach itself. Accessible WC.
- *Ranny Bay and Cliff Walk:* From Penarth follow signs first to the seafront, then to the mini golf. Beginning of the path accessible.
- *Whitmore Bay:* In front of the Pleasure Park at Barry Island. Beach, promenade and WC accessible.

WEST GLAMORGAN

- *Aberavon:* Promenade and slipway access to sandy beach.
- *Caswell Bay:* Slipway leads down to sandy beach.
- *Langland Bay :* Esplanade.
- *Port Eynon:* Car park on edge of beach, slipway leads down to sand.
- *Swansea:* Seafront promenade accessible from Mumbles to the Marina.

GWYNEDD

- *Aberconwy District:* All the beaches and promenades in the Aberconwy district have fairly easy access for wheelchairs.
- *Pwllheli:* Starsplash at Butlins Starcoast World.
- *Trearddur Bay:* Beach on Anglesey has good parking, accessible WC and a ramp to the sandy beach.

Theatres, Cinemas and Concert Halls

There are a number of new theatres and halls in Wales that offer good access and facilities for disabled people, and many of the older establishments are beginning to think about facilities for people with physical and sensory disabilities. But even in the best theatres and halls facilities are limited and prior arrangements are often necessary, so if possible telephone to check.

CLWYD

● *Colwyn Bay:*
Canolfan Colwyn, Colwyn Leisure Centre, Eirias Park. Tel (0492) 533223
Harlequin Marionette Theatre, Rhos on Sea. *WC not accessible but public WC nearby.*
Tel (0492) 48166
Prince of Wales Theatre, Abergele Road.
Tel (0492) 532668

● *Mold:*
Theatr Clwyd. Tel (0352) 55114

● *Rhyl:*
Library Arts Centre, Church Road.
Tel (0745) 353814
New Pavilion Theatre (opening summer 1991).
A new theatre designed to be fully accessible.
Tel (0745) 353814

● *St Asaph:*
St Asaph Cathedral. Tel (0745) 583429

● *Wrexham:*
Grove Park Little Theatre, Hill Street.
WC not accessible.
Tel (0978) 351091
Hippodrome Cinema, Hope Street.
Tel (0978) 364479
William Aston Hall, Mold Road.
Tel (0978) 356601

DYFED

● *Aberystwyth:*
Arts Centre, University College of Wales, Penglais.
Tel (0970) 622882
Commodore Cinema, Bath Street.
Prior booking essential.
Tel (0970) 612421

● *Cardigan:*
Theatre Mwldan, Bathouse Street. Tel (0239) 612687

● *Carmarthen:*
Lyric Cinema, King Street. Tel (0267) 232632

● *Milford Haven:*
Torch Theatre, St Peter's Road. Tel (0646) 694192

MID GLAMORGAN

● *Treorchy:*
Parc and Dare Theatre, Station Road, Rhondda. *WC, removable seating to accommodate wheelchairs.*
Tel (0443) 773112

SOUTH GLAMORGAN

● *Cardiff:*
New Theatre, Park Place.
Accessible throughout, space for wheelchair users and companions (reduced charge). Prior booking essential.
Tel (0222) 394844
Sherman Theatre, Senghenydd Road, Cathays
Tel (0222) 230451
St David's Hall, Working Street. Tel (0222) 42611

WEST GLAMORGAN

● *Swansea:*
Brangwyn Hall, The Guildhall.
Side entrance, chairlift - prior arrangement essential.
Tel (0792) 301301
Dylan Thomas Theatre, 7 Gloucester Place.
Tel (0792) 473238
Grand Theatre, Singleton Street. Tel (0792) 462026
Penyrheol Leisure Centre, Pontarddulais Road, Gorseinon. Tel (0792) 897039
Taliesin Arts Centre, University College.
Tel (0792) 296883
Theatr Cwmtawe, Pontardawe Leisure Centre, Ynysderw Road, Pontardawe. Tel (0792) 830111
UCI Cinemas, 10 The Strand.
10-screen cinema, wheelchair access to all, accessible WC.
Tel (0792) 645005

GWENT

● *Cwmbran:*
Congress Theatre, Gwent Square. Tel (0633) 68239

● *Newport:*
Newport Centre, Kingsway. Tel (0633) 841522

THEATRES, CINEMAS AND CONCERT HALLS

GWYNEDD

● *Bangor:*
Cathedral
WC not accessible.
Tel (0248) 354204
Theatre Gwynedd, Deiniol Road.
Tel (0248) 351707
● *Harlech:*
Theatre Ardudwy, Coleg Harlech.
WC not accessible.
Tel (0766) 780667
● *Holyhead:*
Empire Cinema, Stanley Street. Tel (0407) 2093
● *Llandudno:*
Arcadia Theatre, Promenade. Tel (0492) 879771
● *Llangefni:*
Theatr Fach, Pencraif.
WC not accessible.
Tel (0248) 722412
● *Pwllheli:*
Oriel Plas Gwyn, Llanbedrog. Tel (0758) 740763
Stars, Starcoast World, Butlins Holiday World.
Tel (0758) 612112
Town Cinema, Town Hall, Penlan Street.
Tel (0758) 613371

POWYS

● *Machynlleth:*
Theatr Fach Machynlleth, y Tabernacl, Heol
Penrallt. Tel (0654) 3355
● *Newtown:*
Theatr Hafren, Llanidloes Road.
Space for 12 wheelchair users (book in advance);
parking; accessible WC.
Tel (0686) 625007

● *Further Information:*
Arts for Disabled People in Wales has details of
other artistic venues and events.

● *Please contact:*
Arts for Disabled People in Wales, Channel View,
Jim Driscoll Way, The Marl, Grangetown, Cardiff.
Tel (0222) 377885

St Davids Hall, Cardiff.

Sports and leisure centres

As elsewhere in recent years, there has been a proliferation of sports and leisure centres in Wales. Many centres do accommodate disabled participants, although some extend a warmer welcome than others. The Deeside Leisure Centre, for instance, was a winner of the 1986 Accessible Building Award Scheme and is a good model for new centres.

The Sports Council for Wales actively encourages the development of sport for disabled people and has a specialist staff team which produces a comprehensive guide to sports facilities and associations in Wales. The following is a brief summary of the Sports Council for Wales list of centres with basic access to facilities, the activities available, followed by any special provision made for disabled people. Again, you are strongly advised to telephone before your visit to check that facilities are available when you want to use them.

CLWYD

●*Buckley:*
Buckley Sports Centre, Mill Lane.
Badminton, gymnasium, table tennis, weight training, sauna.
WC, lifts/ramps.
Tel (0224) 546458

●*Chirk:*
Ceiriog Junior School, Lloyd Lane.
Multi-gym, sauna, solarium.
WC, changing, ramps/lifts, parking.
Tel (0691) 772331

●*Colwyn Bay:*
Colwyn Leisure Centre, Eirias Park.
Swimming, squash, weight training, outdoor athletics, bowls, basketball, table tennis, archery, netball, five-a-side, uni-hoc.
WC, changing, wheelchairs available.
Tel (0492) 533223/4/5

●*Connah's Quay:*
Connah's Quay Bath, Civic Centre, Deeside.
Swimming, WC, changing, pool chair-lift.
Tel (0244) 819561

Connah's Quay Sports Centre, Golfryn Lane, Deeside.
Gymnasium, squash, table tennis, outdoor tennis, badminton.
Lifts/ramps.
Tel (0244) 813491

●*Corwen:*
Cynwyd Primary School, Ty'n-y-Gotel, Cynwyd.
Tennis, bowls.
WC, lifts/ramps, parking, wheelchairs available.
Tel (0490) 2306

●*Denbigh:*
Denbigh Leisure Centre, Ruthin Road.
Swimming, gymnasium, sauna, solarium.
WC, changing, viewing, chutes/hoists, lifts/ramps, parking wheelchairs allowed on pool side.
Tel (0745) 716311

●*Flint:*
Flint Leisure Centre, Earl Street.
Swimming, table tennis, basketball, archery, bowls, pool.
WC, lifts/ramps.
Tel (0352) 63677/8

●Holywell:
Holywell Leisure Centre, Fron Park.
Swimming, table tennis, Basketball, bowls, snooker.
WC, changing, lifts/ramps.
Tel (0352) 712027

●Mold:
Mold Sports Centre, Wrexham Road.
Weight training, swimming, table tennis, basketball, bowls, squash. WC, changing.
Tel (0352) 56116/7

●Prestatyn:
North Wales Bowls Centre, Ffrith Beach.
WC, ramps onto bowling green.
Tel (0745) 886100
Prestatyn Sports Centre, Princess Avenue
Bowls, archery, pistol shooting, table tennis, squash, netball, tennis.
WC.
Tel (0745) 65632

●Queensferry:
Deeside Leisure Centre, Chester Road West, Deeside
Squash, weight training, badminton, ice skating, tennis, football, bowling, table tennis, refreshments.
WC, viewing, lifts/ramps, parking, induction loop, wheelchair height telephone.
Tel (0244) 812311

●Rhyl:
Rhyl Sports & Recreation Centre, Grange Road.
Swimming, weight training, badminton, squash.
WC, changing, showers, lifts/ramps.
Tel (0745) 343337

●Ruthin:
Brynhyfryd Recreation Centre, Mold Road.
Swimming pool, gymnasium, sauna, solarium, fitness room.
WC, changing, viewing, parking, chutes/hoists, ramps, wheelchairs allowed on poolside.
Tel (0824) 23880

●St Asaph:
St Asaph Sport/Leisure Centre, Upper Denbigh Road.
Squash, weight training, sauna, solarium.
Tel (0745) 583368

●Wrexham: Castell Alun Sports Centre, nr Hope Village.
Badminton, squash, weight training, gymnasium.
WC.
Tel (0978) 760097
Gwyn Evans Pool, Gwersyllt.
Swimming.
WC, changing.
Tel (0978) 754394
Plas Madoc Leisure Centre, Acrefair.
Weight training, swimming, table tennis, squash. WC, family cubicles.
Tel (0978) 821600

Queen's Park Youth Centre, Queensway.
Badminton, football.
WC, lifts/ramps, parking.
Tel (0978) 351274
Queensway Sports Complex, Queensway.
Table tennis, athletics, bowls, squash, soccer.
WC, lifts/ramps.
Tel (0978) 355826
St David's Community School, Rhosnesni Lane.
Swimming.
WC, changing, chutes/hoists.
Tel (0978) 353792
Wrexham Swimming Baths, Bodhyfryd.
Swimming, table tennis, sauna, solarium.
WC, chutes/hoists, lifts/ramps.
Tel (0978) 263795

DYFED

●Aberystwyth:
Plascrug Swimming Pool, Plascrug.
Swimming, tennis, netball, basketball, five-a-side.
WC, changing, chutes/hoists, lifts/ramps, parking.
Tel (0970) 624579

●Carmarthen:
Carmarthen District Leisure Centre, Llansteffan Road, Johnstown.
Swimming, badminton, martial arts, weight training.
WC, changing, lifts/ramps, parking.
Tel (0267) 230874

●Haverfordwest:
Haverfordwest Sports Centre, Queensway.
Badminton, squash, athletics, tennis.
WC, lifts/ramps.
Tel (0437) 5901
Haverfordwest Swimming Pool, Dew Street.
Swimming.
WC, changing, parking.
Tel (0437) 764354

●Milford Haven:
Meads Sports & Leisure Centre, Priory Road.
Swiming, sauna, solarium, bowls, pool, tennis, table tennis, trim trail.
WC, changing, lifts/ramps, parking, wheelchairs allowed at poolside.
Tel (0646) 694011

●Pembroke:
Pembroke Sports Centre, Bush.
Swimming, badminton, squash, tennis, solarium.
WC.
Tel (0646) 683281

●Tenby: Tenby & District Swimming Pool, Marsh Road SA70 8EJ.
Swimming, viewing.
Lifts/ramps.
Tel (0834) 3575

SPORTS AND LEISURE CENTRES

MID GLAMORGAN

● *Abercynon:*
Abercynon Sports Centre, Parc, nr Aberdare.
Swimming, table tennis, badminton, bowls, basketball.
WC, changing.
Tel (0685) 740141

● *Aberdare:*
Aberdare Swimming Pool, Ynys.
Swimming, snooker, sauna, solarium, jacuzzi, steam room.
WC, changing, viewing, lifts/ramps, parking, pool lift.
Tel (0685) 874252
Michael Sobell Sports Centre, Ynys.
Badminton, bowls, archery, basketball, table tennis.
WC, lifts/ramps.
Tel (0685) 874323

● *Bedwas:*
Bedwas Community College, Old Newport Road.
Swimming, tennis, rugby.
WC, changing, lifts/ramps.
Tel (0222) 852540

● *Bridgend:*
Bridgend Recreation Centre, Newbridge Fields.
Swimming, badminton, bowls, archery, table tennis, basketball.
WC, changing, lifts/ramps, parking.
Tel (0656) 657491

● *Caerphilly:* Caerphilly Recreation Centre, Virginia Park.
Swimming, squash, weight training, health suite.
WC, chutes/hoists, parking.
Tel (0222) 851845

● *Llantrisant:*
Llantrisant Leisure Centre, Southgate Park.
Swimming, badminton, squash, volleyball, sauna, bowls, table games.
WC, changing, chutes/hoists, lifts/ramps.
Tel (0443) 228528

● *Maesteg:*
Maesteg Sports Centre.
Badminton, basketball, table tennis.
WC, changing, lifts/ramps.
Tel (0656) 737121

● *Merthyr Tydfil:*
Dowlais Community Centre, Station Road, Dowlais.
Badminton, table tennis, archery, weight training.
WC, parking.
Tel (0685) 77688
Gurnos Community Centre, Spruce Tree Grove, Gurnos Estate.
Badminton, archery, table tennis, pool.
WC, parking.
Tel (0685) 5284

Rhydycar Sports & Leisure Centre, Rhydycar.
Badminton, basketball, archery, bowls, squash, table tennis, weight training.
WC, changing, lifts/ramps, parking.
Tel (0685) 71491

● *New Tredegar:*
New Tredegar Sports Hall, Grove Park.
Table tennis, multi-gym.
WC.
Tel (0443) 875586

● *Pontycymmer:*
Garw Valley Centre, Old Station Yard.
Table tennis, bowls.
WC, parking.
Tel (0656) 870886

● *Pontypridd:*
Hawthorn Comprehensive Swimming Pool, School Lane, Hawthorn.
Swimming.
WC, changing, lifts/ramps, wheelchairs available.
Tel (0443) 841321
Hawthorn Leisure & Recreation Centre, Fairfield Lane, Hawthorn.
Bowls, badminton, table tennis, basketball, multi-gym, sauna, solarium.
WC, changing, lifts/ramps.
Tel (0443) 843406
Llantwit Fardre Sports Centre, Central Park, Church Village.
Table tennis, badminton, mult-gym, volleyball, netball, basketball, squash, indoor hockey, indoor cricket, football.
Tel (0443) 201722

● *Pyle:*
Pyle & District Leisure Centre, Helig Fan.
Swimming.
WC, chutes/hoists, chair lift.
Tel (0656) 744019

● *Rhondda:*
Ferndale Joint User Swimming Pool, Maerdy.
Swimming, weight training.
WC, changing, viewing.
Tel (0443) 755412
Rhondda Sports Centre, Gelligaled Park, Ystrad.
Swimming, badminton, squash, bowls, archery, rifle shooting, basketball, weight training, table tennis, dance.
WC, changing, lifts/ramps, parking.
Tel (0443) 434093

● *Tonyrefail:*
Tonyrefail Swimming Pool, Ton y Bryn Park.
Swimming, sauna, multi-gym.
WC, changing, chutes/hoists.
Tel (0443) 670578

● *Treharris:* Edwardsville Baths, Edwardsville.
Swimming.
WC, changing, parking.
Tel (0443) 411757
Treharris Community Centre, Perrott Street.
Table tennis, archery, pool, darts.
WC. Tel (0443) 411201

SOUTH GLAMORGAN

● *Barry:*
Barry Leisure Centre, Greenwood Street.
Swimming, bowls, basketball, table tennis.
WC, changing, lifts/ramps.
Tel (0446) 744770
Barry YMCA, New Centre, Court Road.
Weight training, martial arts, football.
WC, lifts/ramps, wheelchairs available.
Tel (0446) 735449
Holm View Centre, Skomer View, Gibbonsdown.
Badminton, squash, weight training.
WC, parking, wheelchairs available.
Tel (0446) 700258
● *Cardiff:*
Canton Community Hall, Leckwith Road.
Table tennis, basketball.
WC, changing.
Tel (0222) 344699
Channel View Recreation & Community Centre,
Jim Driscoll Way, Grangetown CF1 7NF.
Badminton, weight training, squash, sauna.
WC, lifts/ramps.
Tel (0222) 394317
Eastern Leisure Centre, Llanrumney.
Swimming, weight training, badminton, bowls, archery,
table tennis, basketball.
WC, changing, lifts/ramps, parking.
Tel (0222) 796616
Fairwater Leisure Centre, off Waterhall Road,
Fairwater.
Swimming, badminton, trampolining, archery, bowls,
conditioning, table tennis, basketball.
WC, changing, lifts/ramps.
Tel (0222) 552210
Heath Sports Centre, King George V Drive, Heath.
Badminton, conditioning, pitch and putt.
Changing, parking.
Tel (0222) 755607
Llanishen Leisure Centre, Tŷ Glas Avenue,
Llanishen.
Swimming, squash, weight training, snooker.
WC, changing, lifts/ramps, parking, wheelchairs
available.
Tel (0222) 762411

Pentwyn Leisure Centre, Bryn Celyn Road.
Badminton, table tennis, basketball.
WC, changing.
Tel (0222) 549211
Plasnewydd Community Hall, Shakespeare Street.
Table tennis.
WC, changing.
Tel (0222) 751235
Splott Swimming Pool, Muirton Road, Tremorfa.
Swimming.
WC, changing, chutes/hoists, pool chair lift.
Tel (0222) 462548
National Sports Centre for Wales, Sophia Gardens.
Swimming, archery, badminton, bowls, netball,
basketball, table tennis, shooting, tennis.
Wheelchair dancing, WC, lifts/ramps, parking,
accommodation, braille maps.
Tel (0222) 397571
St Mellons Community Hall, Crickhowell Road.
Weight training, table tennis, pool, bowls, basketball.
WC, changing.
Tel (0222) 793895
Star Recreation & Community Centre, Splott,
Road, Splott.
Weight training, table tennis, trampolining, squash,
basketball.
WC, changing, lifts/ramps.
Tel (0222) 484637
Wales Empire Pool, Wood Street.
Swimming, conditioning, table tennis, pool, Turkish
baths.
WC, changing, lifts/ramps.
Tel (0222) 382296
Western Leisure Centre, Caerau Lane, Ely.
Swimming, badminton, bowls, archery, conditioning,
table tennis, basketball.
WC, changing, parking.
Tel (0222) 593592
● *Cowbridge:*
Cowbridge Leisure Centre, Bear Field, Broadshoard.
Table tennis, conditioning, basketball, bowls.
WC, lifts/ramps.
Tel (0446) 5533
● *Llantwit Major:*
Llanilltud Leisure Centre, Ham Lane East.
Swimming, sauna.
WC, changing.
Tel (0446) 793947
● *Penarth:*
Cogan Leisure Centre, Andrew Road, Cogan.
Swimming, basketball, table tennis, conditioning.
WC, changing, lifts/ramps, wheelchairs available, pool
chair-lift.
Tel (0222) 700717

WEST GLAMORGAN

●*Neath:*
Cwrt Herbert Sports Pavilion, Neath Abbey Road.
Changing, toilet and shower facilities for field sports, cafe and bar. Tel (0639) 635013
Dyfed Road Baths, Dyfed Road.
Swimming, weight training, squash.
Changing, viewing, chutes/hoists, lifts/ramps, parking, induction loop, wheelchairs available.
Tel (0639) 2827

●*Pontardawe:*
Pontardawe Leisure Centre, Parc Ynysderw.
Weight training, squash, badminton, solarium.
WC, changing, lifts/ramps, wheelchairs available.
Tel (0792) 830111

●*Port Talbot:*
Afan Lido Sports Centre, Aberavon Beach.
Swimming, badminton, squash, canoeing, dance, football, martial arts, keep fit, weight training, netball, yoga, table tennis.
WC, changing, viewing, lifts/ramps, parking.
Tel (0639) 884141

●*Swansea:*
Dillwyn Llewellyn Leisure Centre, John Street, Cockett.
Badminton, weight training, table tennis, basketball, bowls.
WC, changing, lifts/ramps, parking.
Tel (0792) 585956
Morfa Stadium, Upper Bank, Landore.
Athletics, football, netball, darts, table tennis, bowls, archery, weight training.
Wheelchair activities, WC, lift/ramps.
Tel (0792) 476578
Morriston Community Sports Centre, Cwmrhydyceirw, Morriston.
Swimming, badminton, short tennis, basketball, volleyball, table tennis.
Changing.
Tel (0792) 797082
Olchfa Community Centre, Sketty.
Swimming, badminton, short tennis, basketball, volleyball, five-a-side football, table tennis.
Changing.
Tel (0792) 205604
Pentrehafod Community Sports Centre, Hafod.
Swimming, badminton, basketball, volleyball, table tennis.
Tel (0792) 41935
Penyrheol Community School & Leisure Centre, Penyrheol, Gorseinon.
Swimming, badminton, gymnasium, table tennis, tennis, multi-gym, sauna.
WC, parking.
Tel (0792) 897039

Swansea Leisure Centre, Oystermouth Road.
Swimming, badminton, weight training, squash, table tennis, bowls, cricket, martial arts.
WC, changing, lifts/ramps, parking, wheelchairs available.
Tel (0792) 649126

GWENT

●*Abergavenny:*
Abergavenny Leisure Centre, Old Hereford Road.
Swimming, badminton, squash, table tennis, basketball.
WC, changing, lifts/ramps, parking.
Tel (0873) 77444

●*Abersychan:*
Abersychan Leisure Centre, Manor Road.
Badminton, table tennis, basketball.
WC, lifts/ramps.
Tel (0495) 773140

●*Abertillery:*
Abertillery Community Centre, Gelli Crug School.
Badminton, tennis, hockey, football, rugby.
WC, lifts/ramps, parking, wheelchairs available.
Tel (0495) 217111

●*Blackwood:*
Cefn Fforest Sports Centre, Cefn Fforest.
Swimming, squash, sauna, solarium, jacuzzi.
WC, changing, lifs/ramps.
Tel (0495) 830567

●*Blaenafon:* Blaenafon Recreation Centre, Recreation Road.
Swimming, sauna, solarium, squash.
WC, changing, lifts/ramps.
Tel (0495) 790646

●*Brynmawr:*
Nantyglo Leisure Centre, Pond Road.
Swimming, badminton, weight training, table tennis, basketball.
WC, changing.
Tel (0495) 310785

●*Caldicot:* Caldicot Community College and Leisure Centre.
Swimming, badminton, squash, basketball, table tennis, sauna, solarium.
WC, changing, lifts/ramps, parking.
Tel (0291) 420375

●*Chepstow:*
Chepstow & District Leisure Centre, St Kingsmark Comprehensive School, Crossway Green.
Swimming, badminton, basketball, sauna, solarium.
WC, changing, lifts/ramps, parking.
Tel (02912) 3832/3701

● Cwmbran:
Cwmbran Stadium, Henllys Way.
Swimming, badminton, bowls, weight training, athletics, table tennis, sauna, solarium.
WC, changing, parking.
Tel (06333) 66192/66193
Fairwater Leisure Centre, Tŷ Gwyn Way, Fairwater.
Swimming, badminton, squash, table tennis, basketball.
WC, lift/ramps, parking.
Tel (06333) 72811
Llantarnam Leisure Centre, Llantarnam Road.
Swimming, badminton, table tennis, basketball.
WC, lift/ramps.
Tel (06333) 2832

● Ebbw Vale:
Ebbw Vale Leisure Centre, Civic Centre Site.
Swimming, weight training, badminton, table tennis, basketball.
WC, changing, lifts/ramps, parking.
Tel (0495) 303766

● Monmouth:
Monmouth Leisure Centre, Old Dixton Road.
Swimming, badminton, table tennis, tennis, hockey, football.
WC, lift/ramps.
Tel (0600) 714646

● Newbridge:
Newbridge Leisure Centre, Bridge Street.
Badminton, squash, weight training, table tennis, basketball.
WC, lifts/ramps.
Tel (0495) 248100

● Newport:
Bettws Leisure Centre, Bettws
Swimming, table tennis, badminton, basketball.
WC.
Tel (0633) 855420
Liswerry Leisure Centre, Nash Road.
Swimming, badminton, table tennis, basketball, multi-gym.
WC, chutes/hoists, lifts/ramps.
Tel (0633) 274919
Newport Centre, Kingsway.
Swimming, badminton, netball, weight training, table tennis, bowls, sauna, solarium.
Remedial hydrotherapy bath, WC, changing, lifts/ramps.
Tel (0633) 841522
Underwood Leisure Centre, Llantarnam.
Swimming, badminton, bowls, squash.
WC, lifts/ramps.
Tel (0633) 412090

● Pontllanfraith:
Pontllanfraith Leisure Centre.
Badminton, table tennis, squash, basketball.
WC, lifts/ramps.
Tel (0495) 224562

● Pontypool:
Pontypool Leisure Centre, Pontypool Park.
Swimming, badminton, table tennis, weight training, snooker, skiing.
WC, lifts/ramps, parking.
Tel (04955) 55764

● Risca:
Risca Leisure Centre, Comprehensive School, Pontymason.
Swimming, badminton, squash, table tennis, basketball.
WC, lifts/ramps.
Tel (0633) 613983

● Tredegar:
Tredegar Leisure Centre, Stable Lane.
Swimming, badminton, table tennis, basketball, sauna, solarium.
WC, changing, lifts/ramps.
Tel (0495) 253554/711781

GWYNEDD

● Amlwch:
Amlwch Leisure Centre, Anglesey.
Swimming, badminton, squash, mini tennis, shuffle board, table tennis, basketball, netball, volleyball, weight training.
WC, changing.
Tel (0407) 830060

● Bangor:
Arfon Sports Hall, Ffriddoedd Road.
Badminton, five-a-side football, netball, table tennis, basketball.
WC, parking, steps to balcony.
Tel (0248) 351697
Bangor Swimming Pool, Garth Road.
Swimming, bowls, solarium.
Changing, chutes/hoists, lifts/ramps.
Tel (0248) 370600

● Caernarfon:
Arfon Leisure Centre, Bethel Road.
Swimming, badminton, squash, bowls, solarium.
WC, changing, lifts/ramps.
Tel (2086) 76451
Plas Menai, National Watersports Centre, Llanfairisgaer.
Outdoor/water sports, swimming, table tennis.
Wheelchair dancing, WC, changing, viewing, lifts/ramps, parking, 'Able Sailor' rig available.
Residential courses, accommodation.
Tel (0248) 670964

● Holyhead:
Holyhead Leisure Centre, Anglesey.
Swimming, table tennis, archery, volleyball, basketball, netball, bowls squash, weight training, snooker, darts, trampoline.
WC, changing, viewing, lifts/ramps.
Tel (0407) 4111

SPORTS AND LEISURE CENTRES

●*Llandudno:*

Llandudno Swimming pool, Mostym Broadway.
Swimming.
Changing, pool lift.
Tel (0492) 78838

●*Llangefni:*

Plas Arthur Leisure Centre, Anglesey.
Swimming, badminton, bowls, basketball, volleyball,
squash, mini-tennis.
Slope for entry into learner pool.
Tel (0492) 78838

●*Llanrwst:*

Llanrwst Swimming Pool, Watling Street.
Swimming.
WC, lifts/ramps.
Tel (0492) 640921

●*Pwllheli:*

Canolfan Hamdden Dwyfor, Lon Caerdydd.
Swimming pool.
Lift, ramps throughout.
Tel (0758) 613437

●*Tywyn:*

Bro Dysynni Leisure Centre, High Street.
Swimming, badminton, netball, five-a-side football,
volleyball, basketball, tennis, golf, table tennis, squash,
bowls.
Changing, chutes/hoists, lifts/ramps, parking, induction
loop, wheelchairs available.
Tel (0654) 710167

POWYS

●*Brecon:*

Brecon Swimming Pool, Penlan.
Swimming.
WC, changing, parking.
Tel (0874) 3677
Gwerhyfed Sports Hall, Three Cocks.
Badminton, basketball, table tennis, conditioning.
Parking.
Tel (04974) 445

●*Builth Wells:* Builth Wells Bowling Club/Sports
Centre, North Road.
Badminton, bowls, archery, table tennis, basketball,
conditioning.
WC, changing, parking.
Tel (0982) 552324

●*Crickhowell:* Crickhowell Sports Centre.
Badminton, table tennis, conditioning.
WC, changing, parking.
Tel (0873) 810997

●*Llandrindod Wells:*

Llandrindod Wells & District Leisure Centre,
Dyffryn Road.
Swimming, badminton, archery, bowls, conditioning,
table tennis.
WC, changing, chutes/hoists, parking.
Tel (0597) 4249

●*Llanfyllin:*

Llanfyllin Sports Centre.
Swimming, bowls, conditioning, table tennis.
WC, changing, parking.
Tel (069184) 391

●*Llanidloes:*

Llanidloes & District Sports Centre, Llangurig Road.
Swimming, bowls, table tennis, conditioning.
WC, changing, parking.
Tel (05512) 2871

● *Machynlleth:*

Bro Dyfi Leisure Centre, Aberystwyth Road.
Swimming, indoor bowls, sports hall, climbing, sauna,
basketball.
WC, changing, parking, lift.
Tel: (0654) 703300

●*Newtown:*

Maldwyn Sports Centre, Plantation Lane.
Swimming, badminton, bowls, table tennis, conditioning.
WC, changing, parking. Pool temperature cool.
Tel (0686) 28771

●*Presteigne:*

East Radnor Sports Centre, Broad Axe Lane.
Swimming, badminton, squash, tennis, cricket, hockey,
rugby, football.
WC, viewing, parking.
Tel (0554) 260302

●*Sennybridge:*

Defynnog Swimming Pool.
Swimming.
Tel (0874) 636512

●*Welshpool:*

Armoury Recreation Centre, Brook Street.
Bowls, table tennis, conditioning, basketball, pool.
WC.
Tel (0938) 554143
Welshpool Baths.
Swimming, conditioning.
WC, changing, parking.
Tel (0938) 2935

●**Ystradgynlais:**
Maesydderwen School, Tudor Street.
Swimming, badminton, weight training, aerobics, dance.
WC, changing, chutes/hoists, lifts/ramps, parking,
wheelchairs, available. One night a week set aside
especially for disabled people.
Tel (0792) 842115

Ystradgynlais Swimming Pool, Ystradgynlais.
Swimming.
WC, changing, lifts.
Tel (0792) 844854

Spectating

The following sports grounds provide some facilities for visitors with disabilities. Please telephone before visiting to ensure that the facilities you need are available.

SOUTH GLAMORGAN

●*Cardiff:*
Cardiff City Football Association Ltd, Ninian Park
CF1 8SX.
Tel (0222) 398636/7/8
Cardiff Rugby Football Club, Cardiff Arms Park,
Westgate Street CF1 1JC.
Special enclosure for wheelchair spectators.
Tel (0222) 383546
Sophia Gardens Cricket Ground.
Tel (0222) 387367

WEST GLAMORGAN

●*Swansea:*
St Helens Cricket Ground.
Tel (0792) 466321
Swansea City Football Club Ltd, Vetch Field,
Glamorgan Street SA1 3SY.
Tel (0792) 474114

Riding for disabled people

Riding Associations for disabled people are well represented in Wales and local groups welcome visitors. Contact representatives of local associations listed below for details of group activities.

Riding for the Disabled Association Local Groups:

CLWYD

● *Abergele:* (West Clwyd)
Sirior Goch Farm, Betws-yn-Rhos, Abergele LL22 8PL.
Contact: Mrs J Hunter.
Tel (0745) 832237

● *Deeside:*
Pengwibant, Meretyn Downing Lane, Whitford, nr Holywell CH8 9EP.
Contact: Mrs G Morgan.
Tel (0745) 560795

● *Denbigh:* (Greenfield)
Trefnant, Denbigh LL16 5UE.
Contact: Mrs E Griffith.
Tel (074574) 633

● *Llangollen:* (Dyffryn Ceiriog)
Buarth Cynfor, Glyn Ceiriog, Llangollen LL20 7HB.
Contact: Mrs T Sopwith.
Tel (069172) 474

● *St Asaph:* (Waen)
2 The Roe, St Asaph.
Contact: Mrs D Carr.
Tel (0745) 584844

● *Vale of Clwyd:*
Tyn-y-Waen, Glasfryn, Corwen LL21 0RY.
Contact: Mrs O Greenwood.
Tel (049082) 482

● *Wrexham:* Clwyd Special Riding Centre, Llanfynydd LL11 5HN.
Contact: Mrs E Rollinson.
Tel (0352) 770446

DYFED

● *Aberystwyth:*
Tŷ Isaf, Llanilar, Aberystwyth SY23 4NP.
Contact: Mrs S N Wulstan.
Tel (097421) 229

● *Carmarthen:* (Castell Howard)
Banc Farm, Abergorlech, Carmarthen SA32 7SR.
Contact: Mrs C Harmer.
Tel (0267) 202228

● *Lamphey:* (Pembrokeshire A)
Hillside House, Freshwater East, Lamphey SA71 5LB.
Contact: Mrs M Phillips.
Tel (0646) 672496

● *Llanelli:*
Yr Olygfa, The Graig, Burry Port SA16 0BZ.
Contact: Mrs B Parry.
Tel (05546) 5215

● *Llangadog:*
Blaen Cwm, Llanddeusant, Llangadog SA19 9YF.
Contact: Mrs A Williams.
Tel (05504) 287

● *Narberth:* (Pembrokeshire E)
Hollybush Farm, Reynalton, Narberth.
Contact: Mrs C Tegg.
Tel (0834) 861110

● *North Pembrokeshire & Cardiganshire:*
Siop-y-Swgar, 28 High Street, St Dogmael's SA43 1EJ.
Contact: Mrs M E Brown.
Tel (0239) 612036

● *St David's:* (Pembrokeshire C)
Tŷ Olaf, Mount Gardens, St David's, Haverfordwest SA62 6BS.
Contact: Mrs R Liggitt.
Tel (0437) 720885

● *Tenby:* (Pembrokeshire B)
Tŷ Newydd, St Florence, Tenby SA70 8NB.
Contact: Mrs M Birch.
Tel (0834) 871213

RIDING ASSOCIATIONS

MID GLAMORGAN

●*Aberdare:* (Green Meadow)
Green Meadow Riding Centre, Country Park,
Aberdare CF44 7PT.
Contact: Mrs S Williams.
Tel (0685) 874961

●*Bridgend:*
Longacre Farm, Coity, Bridgend CF35 6BN.
Contact: Mrs J Ladbroke.
Tel (0656) 653502

●*Treorchy:* (Tŷ Draw)
146 Wyndham Street, Tynewydd, Treorchy CF42 5BS.
Contact: Mrs A Evans.
Tel (0443) 771614

SOUTH GLAMORGAN

●*Cardiff:* (Heath)
32 St Albans Avenue, Heath, Cardiff CF4 4AT.
Contact: Mrs P Grey.
Tel (0222) 693582
(Lindens School) 24 Nant Fawr Road, Cyncoed,
Cardiff CF2 6JR.
Contact: Mrs M Salisbury.
Tel (0222) 754830

●*Tychwyth:* (Cardiff & South Glamorgan)
The Downs, St Nicholas, nr Cardiff CF5 6SB.
Contact: Mrs A Richards.
Tel (0222) 593566

●*Cowbridge:* (St Quentins)
Lake Farm, St Athan Road, Cowbridge.
Contact: Mrs H W Lewis.
Tel (0446) 33366

●*Dinas Powys:* (Dinas Powys A)
3 Murch Crescent, Dinas Powys.
Contact: Mrs P Vincent.
Tel (0222) 514216
(Dinas Powys B) 32 Millbrook Road, Dinas Powys
CF6 4DA.
Contact: Mrs J Masrch.
Tel (0222) 513395
(Dinas Powys C) 30 Greenfield Avenue, Dinas
Powys CF6 4BW.
Contact: Mrs C S Corp.
Tel (0222) 515609

WEST GLAMORGAN

●*Neath:* (Pant-y-Sais)
The Cottage, 49 Hill Road, Neath Abbey, Neath
SA10 7NW.
Contact: Mrs M Smith.
Tel (0792) 813193

●*Swansea:* (Swansea Red Cross)
Frogpool, Nicholaston, Penmaen, Swansea
SA3 2HL.
Contact: Mrs J Sullivan.
Tel (0792) 371622

GWENT

●*Abergavenny:* (Neville Hall Hospital)
Occupational Therapy Department, Pen-y-Fal
Hospital, Abergavenny.
Contact: Mrs N Barrell.
Tel (0873) 2343 ext 277

●*Chepstow:* (Devauden Driving)
Great House Farm, Wolvesnewton, Chepstow
NP6 6NY.
Contact: Dr A Jacques.
Tel (02915) 224

●*Gilwern:*
Pen y Cwm Special School, Old Rectory
Farmhouse, Maesygwartha, Gilwern,
Abergavenny NP7 0EY.
Contact: Mrs H Lipscombe.
Tel (0873) 830244

●*Newport:* (Catsash)
Draenllwyn, Catsash, Newport NP6 1JQ.
Contact: Miss E Haines.
Tel (0633) 412950
(Womble) 53 Medway Road, Bettws, Newport
NP9 6XZ.
Contact: Miss J E A Crowley.
Tel (0633) 858844

●*Pontypool:* (Clytha)
Tŷ Isha, Mamhilad, Pontypool.
Contact: Mrs K Hayman-Joyce.
Tel (0495) 28573

●*Trellech:*
Well Cottage, Earlswood, nr Chepstow
NP6 6AW.
Contact: Mrs G Wells.
Tel (02917) 346

GWYNEDD

● *Aberconwy:*
Bryn Corach, Sychnant Pass Road, Conwy
LL32 8AQ.
Contact: Mrs H Cave.
Tel (049263) 6339

●*Bangor:* (Treborth)
9 Lon y Meillion, Bangor LL57 2LE.
Contact: Mrs R F E Axford.
Tel (0248) 362838

●*Beddgelert:* (Hafod y Llyn)
The Old Vicarage, Beddgelert, LL55 4UY.
Contact: Mrs G Brown.
Tel (076686) 4467

●*Conwy:* (Wern y Wylan)
47 Albert Drive, Deganwy, Conwy LL31 9RH.
Contact: Mrs E Futyan.
Tel (0492) 82833

●*Dolgellau:* (Hencwrt Hall School)
Rhydymain, nr Dolgellau LL40 2AR.
Contact: Miss C Wynne Evans.
Tel (034141) 641
(Meirionnydd Red Cross) Cefn-y-Maes, Brithdir,
Dolgellau LL40 2RP.
Contact: Mrs S Yorke.
Tel (0341) 41248

●*Llandudno:* (Ysgol Gogarth)
87 Victoria Drive, Llandudno Junction LL31 9PG.
Contact: Mrs A Curry.
Tel (0492) 84486

●*Ynys Môn:* (Anglesey)
Penlon, Llandegfan, Anglesey.
Contact: Mrs J Davies.
Tel (0248) 713859

POWYS

●*Builth Wells:* (Brecknock)
Pen-y-Waun, Llanafan Fawr, Builth Wells LD2 3LR.
Contact: Mrs T Newberry.
Tel (05912) 326

●*Newtown:* (Camnant Dolfor)
Camnant, Dolfor, Newtown SY16 4BS.
Contact: Miss M Coyne.
Tel (0597) 83271

●*Welshpool:* (Montgomery Area Red Cross)
Glenfryn, Belan School Lane, Welshpool SY21 8SF.
Contact: Mrs E Ogilvy.
Tel (0938) 552701

Local facilities

While tourist attractions are now beginning to take disabled visitors seriously, access to facilities in the community at large still presents problems. Far too few banks, post offices, restaurants, pubs and toilets are accessible or have facilities for disabled people. And the problem is exacerbated by poor publicity: those with disabled facilities rarely broadcast the fact.

The following listing will at least begin to put the record straight. The information in this section has been the most difficult to collect, so if some of the county entries seem thin this may be because we have yet to discover accessible facilities (on the other hand, they simply may not exist). This is one area where you can help us. If you discover that perfect, accessible place to eat, drink or perform any other day-to-day activities, please let us know.

Banks

CLWYD

● *Abergele:*
Barclays, 67 Market Street. Tel (0745) 832137
Midland, Market Street. Tel (0745) 832227
● *Buckley:*
Barclays, Bistre Avenue. Tel (0244) 544880
● *Colwyn Bay:*
Barclays, 40 Conway Road. Tel (0492) 860220
● *Denbigh:*
Barclays, 10 Hall Square. Tel (0745) 713522
● *Flint:*
Barclays, 19 Church Street. Tel (0352) 662022
● *Mold:*
Barclays, 38 High Street. Tel (0352) 700300
● *Old Colwyn:*
Barclays, 372 Abergele Road. Tel (0492) 860220
● *Prestatyn:*
Barclays, 128 High Street. Tel (0745) 343556
● *Queensferry:*
Barclays, 10 Station Road. Tel (0352) 662022
● *Rhos on Sea:*
Barclays, 18 Everard Road. Tel (0492) 860220

● *Rhyl:*
Barclays, 68 High Street. Tel (0745) 343556
● *Ruthin:*
National Westminster, St Peter's Square.
Tel (0824) 22009
● *Wrexham:*
National Westminster, 31 Lord Street.
Tel (0978) 353344

DYFED

● *Aberystwyth:*
Barclays, 26 Terrace Road. Tel (0970) 612731
● *Carmarthen:*
Barclays, 9 Guildhall Square. Tel (0267) 232444
TSB, 5 Blue Street SA31 1PR. Tel (0267) 221330
Accessible WC
● *Milford Haven:*
Barclays, 16 Hamilton Terrace. Tel (0646) 697131
● *Narberth:*
Barclays, 5 St James Street. Tel (0834) 860323
● *Newcastle Emlyn:*
Barclays, 8 Cawdor Terrace. Tel (0239) 710326
● *St Clear's:*
Barclays, Pentre Road. Tel (0994) 230424

LOCAL FACILITIES

MID GLAMORGAN

●*Aberdare:*
National Westminster, 26 Victoria Street.
Tel (0685) 874347
TSB, 27 Victoria Square, Tel (0685) 876016
●*Caerphilly:*
TSB, 42a Cardiff Road. Tel (0222) 866837
National Westminster, 19 Cardiff Road.
Tel (0222) 869935
Lloyds, 21 Cardiff Road. Tel (0222) 860521
●*Maesteg:*
National Westminster, 15 Talbot Street.
Tel (0656) 737212
●*Merthyr Tydfil:*
TSB, 16 New Market Walk. Tel (0685) 721940

SOUTH GLAMORGAN

●*Barry:*
National Westminster, 117 Holton Road.
Tel (0446) 747225
TSB, 120 Holton Road. Tel (0446) 735730
●*Cardiff:*
Barclays, 121 Queen Street. Tel (0222) 222633
National Westminster, 96 Queen Street.
Tel (0222) 394911
National Westminster, 41 Splott Road.
Tel (0222) 462921
National Westminster, 185 Clare Road,
Grangetown. Tel (0222) 372188
National Westminster, 50 Station Road, Llanishen.
Tel (0222) 750611
National Westminster, 277 Cowbridge Road East,
Canton. Tel (0222) 394101
TSB, 30 Clifton Street. Tel (0222) 462225
TSB, 1 Queen Street. Tel (0222) 382727
Barclays, 47a Cardiff Road, Llandaff.
Tel (0222) 239055
Barclays, 34 Station Road, Llanishen.
Tel (0222) 765211
●*Llantwit Major:*
Barclays, Commercial Street. Tel (0446) 794221
●*Penarth:*
Barclays, 2 Windsor Road. Tel (0222) 704388
●*Radyr:*
National Westminster, Station Road.
Tel (0222) 842512
●*Rumney:*
National Westminster, 763 Newport Road.
Tel (0222) 777355

WEST GLAMORGAN

●*Port Talbot:*
Lloyds, Station Road. Tel (0639) 891401
●*Swansea:*
Barclays, Gower Road, Killay. Tel (0792) 201376
Barclays, Swansea Enterprise Park. Tel (0792) 310300
Lloyds, Beaumont House, Charter Court, Pheonix
Way, Swansea Enterprise Park. Tel (0792) 310532
National Westminster, 21 Woodfield Street,
Morriston. Tel (0792) 771800
National Westminster, 528 Mumbles Road,
Mumbles. Tel (0792) 361561
TSB, 6/14 Pontarddulais Road, Gorseinon.
Tel (0792) 892555
TSB, 32 Uplands Crescent, Uplands.
Tel (0792) 646502
Lloyds, 113 High Street, Gorseinon.
Tel (0792) 897071

GWENT

●*Abergavenny:*
Barclays, 57 Frogmore Street. Tel (0873) 5911
TSB, 23 High Street. Tel (0873) 2272
●*Abertillery:*
National Westminster, 1 Somerset Street.
Tel (0495) 212591
●*Caldicot:*
Barclays, 64a Newport Road. Tel (0291) 425522
●*Chepstow:*
Barclays, Beaufort Square. Tel (0291) 270231
TSB, Beaufort Square. Tel (0291) 627467
Accessible WC
●*Cwmbran:*
National Westminster, 41 Gwent Square.
Tel (0633) 369512
TSB, 7/8 General Rees Square. Tel (0633) 872441
●*Ebbw Vale:*
National Westminster, 14 Market Street.
Tel (0495) 302263
TSB, 25 Market Street. Tel (0495) 303163
●*Newport:*
TSB, 67 Bridge Street. Tel (0633) 267023
TSB, 110-112 Chepstow Road, Maindee.
Tel (0633) 257756
●*Pontypool:*
TSB, 10 Hanbury Road. Tel (0495) 763118
●*Risca:*
National Westminster, 70 Tredegar Street. Tel
(0633) 612276

GWYNEDD

●*Amlwch:*
Barclays, 17 Salem Street, Anglesey.
Tel (0407) 830434
●*Bala:*
Barclays, 68 High Street. Tel (0678) 520315
●*Barmouth:*
Barclays, High Street. Tel (0341) 280408
National Westminster, Bank Place.
Tel (0341) 280443
●*Benllech:*
Barclays, Glanrafon Bach. Tel (0248) 852691
●*Blaenau Ffestiniog:*
Barclays, 17a High Street. Tel (0766) 830237
●*Dolgellau:*
Barclays, Llys Owain. Tel (0341) 422453
●*Holyhead:*
Barclays, 65 Market Square, Anglesey.
Tel (0407) 762223
●*Llandudno:*
Barclays, 84 Mostyn Street. Tel (0492) 860220
●*Llangefni:*
Barclays, 24 Church Street, Anglesey.
Tel (0248) 750052
●*Penygroes:*
Barclays, Tŷ Eryri, Water Street. Tel (0286) 880215
●*Porthmadog:*
Barclays, 70 High Street. Tel (0766) 513177
●*Tywyn:*
National Westminster. Tel (0654) 710231

POWYS

●*Builth Wells:*
Barclays, Broad Street. Tel (0982) 553316
●*Knighton:*
Barclays, 19 Broad Street. Tel (0547) 528337
●*Llanidloes:*
Barclays, 1 Great Oak Street. Tel (0551) 23282
●*Machynlleth:*
Barclays, 4 Pentrerhedyn Street. Tel (0654) 702441
●*Newtown:*
Barclays, 3 Cross Buildings. Tel (0686) 626232
●*Ystradgynlais:*
Lloyds, 14 Commercial Street. Tel (0639) 843243
(access work currently being carried out - scheduled for completion Oct '91)

Post Offices

CLWYD

●*Abergele:*
21 Market Street. Tel (0745) 833149

●*Colwyn Bay:*
46 Princes Drive. Tel (0492) 532453
5 Penrhyn Avenue, Llandrillo-yn-Rhos.
Tel (0492) 44392
●*Holywell:*
50 High Street. Tel (0352) 710389
●*Mold:*
18 Earl Road. Tel (0352) 2083
●*Prestatyn:*
4 King's Avenue. Tel (0745) 4232
●*Rhyl:*
31 Rhyl Coast Road, Brynhedydd. Tel (0745) 353934
2 Water Street. Tel (0745) 343991
●*Ruthin:*
18 St Peter's Square. Tel (0824) 23128
●*Wrexham:*
4 High Street, Overton. Tel (0978) 73201
Chester Road, Gresford. Tel (0978) 832783
12 Dean Road, Rhosnesni. Tel (0978) 261871
59 Wrexham Road, Rhostyllen. Tel (0978) 263472
27 Regent Street. Tel (0978) 356291

DYFED

●*Ammanford:*
4a Quay Street. Tel (0269) 2455
●*Cardigan:*
26 High Street. Tel (0239) 612108
●*Carmarthen:*
9/10 King Street. Tel (0267) 233264
●*Llanelli:*
18 John Street. Tel (0554) 772500
●*Milford Haven:*
95 Robert Street. Tel (0646) 690103
●*Pembroke Dock:*
20 Dimond Street. Tel (0646) 621202
●*Tenby:*
Warren Street. Tel (0834) 3213

MID GLAMORGAN

●*Bridgend:*
Dunraven Place, Wyndham Street. Tel (0656) 650295
●*Porth:*
Porth Street. Tel (0443) 682007
●*Porthcawl:*
86 John Street. Tel (0656) 713650
●*Treorchy:*
21/23 High Street. Tel (0443) 775811

SOUTH GLAMORGAN

●*Barry:*
3/5 Holton Road. Tel (0446) 733608
●*Cardiff:*
47/49 Albany Road. Tel (0222) 483228

234a Cowbridge Road East, Canton.
Tel (0222) 230329
11 Churchill House, Churchill Way.
Tel (0222) 230731
2/4 Hill Street, The Hayes. Tel (0222) 227305
87 Countisbury Avenue, Llanrumney.
Tel (0222) 777154
Merthyr Road, Whitchurch. Tel (0222) 620170
●*Penarth:* 41 Albert Road. Tel (0222) 708478

WEST GLAMORGAN

●*Neath:* 20 Windsor Road. Tel (0639) 643876
●*Port Talbot:*
139 Station Road. Tel (0639) 891432
●*Swansea:*
26 Alexandra Road, Gorseinon. Tel (0792) 892909

GWENT

●*Abergavenny:*
1 St John's Square. Tel (0873) 2833
●*Cwmbran:*
General Rees Square. Tel (0633) 33114
●*Ebbw Vale:* 50 Bethcar Street. Tel (0495) 303742
●*Monmouth:* Priory Street. Tel (0600) 712021
●*Newport:* 9 Bridge Street. Tel (0633) 259484
●*Tredegar:*
Gwent Shopping Precinct. Tel (0495) 252391

GWYNEDD

●*Bangor:* 60 Deiniol Road. Tel (0248) 354444
Ogwen Terrace, Bethesda. Tel (0248) 600495
Hirael. Tel (0248) 362100

●*Barmouth:*
King Edward Street. Tel (0341) 280650
●*Benllech:* Tel (0248) 852321
●*Caernarfon:* Groeslon. Tel (0341) 280650
Pengroes. Tel (0286) 880201
●*Conwy:* 18 Bangor Road. Tel (0492) 592468
●*Dolgarrog:* Conwy Road. Tel (0492) 69239
●*Holyhead:*
13a Boston Street, Anglesey. Tel (0407) 2142
Llanfaethlu, Anglesey. Tel (0407) 730201
●*Llandudno:*
Great Ormes Road. Tel (0492) 875591
14 Vaughan Street. Tel (0492) 875591
●*Llangefni:*
18 Church Street, Anglesey. Tel (0248) 750160
●*Llanrwst:* Station Road. Tel (0492) 640473
●*Menai Bridge:*
Maldwyn, Anglesey. Tel (0248) 713240
●*Porthmadog:* Morfa Bychan. Tel (0766) 512096

POWYS

●*Brecon:* St Mary Street. Tel (0874) 2518
●*Llandrindod Wells:*
Ridgebourne. Tel (0597) 2626
●*Montgomery:* Abermule. Tel (0686) 630201
●*Welshpool:* Dolanog. Tel (0938) 810235
Severn Street. Tel (0938) 2194

VISIT A TOURIST
INFORMATION CENTRE

Places to Eat and Drink

Even the best pub, cafe or restaurant gets crowded. Where possible, you are advised to telephone beforehand to check facilities and perhaps to reserve a space in advance.

Pubs

Many public houses in Wales are reasonably accessible, although few have wheelchair accessible toilets. The following advertise facilities for disabled people.

CLWYD

● *Abergele:*
Yacht, Marine Road, Pensarn. Tel (0745) 824052
● *Graigfechan:*
Three Pigeons Inn. Tel (08242) 3178
● *Gresford:*
Plough Inn, Chester Road, nr Wrexham.
Tel (0978) 661696
● *Halkyn:*
Britannia Inn, Pentre Road. Tel (0352) 780272
● *Wrexham:*
Holly Bush, Cefn y Bedd. Tel (0978) 761716
Squire Yorke, Sontley Road. Tel (0978) 261007

DYFED

● *Llanelli:*
Pheonix, Gorslas, nr Cross Hands. Tel (0269) 844438
● *Llangadog:*
Pont-Aber Inn, Llanddeusant, Llangadog.
Tel (0550) 4202

MID GLAMORGAN

● *Caerphilly:*
Court House Inn, Cardiff Road. Tel (0222) 888120
Rose & Castle, Bedwas Road.Tel (0222) 883306
● *Merthyr Tydfil:*
Great Escape, Nantgwyneth Street, Georgetown.
Tel (0685) 79640
Matchstick Man, Forsythia Close, Gurnos Estate.
Tel (0685) 71088

SOUTH GLAMORGAN

● *Cardiff:*
Cottage Hotel, Sanquahar Street, Adamsdown.
Tel (0222) 461744
Hollybush Inn, Glyncoed Road, Cyncoed.
Tel (0222) 731171
Llanrumney Hall: Ball Road, Llanrumney.
Tel (0222) 777792
Old Cottage, Cherry Orchard Road, Lisvane.
Tel (0222) 747582
Radyr Arms, Station Road, Radyr.
Tel (0222) 843121
Three Arches, Heathwood Road, Llanishen.
Tel (0222) 753831
Village Inn, Croescadarn Road, North Pentwyn.
Tel (0222) 549055
● *Penarth:*
Railway Inn, Plymouth Road. Tel (0222) 705754

WEST GLAMORGAN

● *Swansea:*
Bath Hotel, 296 Oystermouth Road.
Tel (0792) 654231
Marquis Arms, Carmarthen Road, Fforestfach.
Tel (0792) 580805
Penplas, Penplas District Shopping Centre.
Tel (0792) 580923
Traveller's Rest, Samlet Road, Llansamlet.
Tel (0792) 710670

Pubs

GWENT

●*Caerleon:*
Goldcroft Inn, Goldcroft Common.
Tel (0633) 420504
Malthouse Hotel, New Road. Tel (0633) 423687
●*Marshfield:*
Mason Arms, 10 St Mellons Road. Tel (0633) 680308
●*Tredegar:*
Castle, Castle Street. Tel (0495) 254604

GWYNEDD

●*Conwy:*
Y Beddol, Conway Road, Talybont, nr Conwy.
Tel (0492) 69501

●*Deganwy:*
Maggie Murphy's, Pentwyn. Tel (0492) 83695
●*Holyhead:*
Edinburgh Castle Hotel, Anglesey.
Tel (0407) 762015
White Eagle Inn, Rhoscolyn, Anglesey.
Tel (0407) 860267
●*Menai Bridge:*
Gazelle, Anglesey. Tel (0248) 713364
●*Nefyn:*
Bryn Cynan, Morfa Nefyn. Tel (0758) 720879

POWYS

●*Talybont-on-Usk:*
Traveller's Rest. Tel (0874) 87233

Eating Out

Like pubs, many cafes and restaurants in Wales are accessible, although they may not have fully accessible toilets. The following establishments are used by disabled people. As before, we recommend that, if possible, you telephone ahead to check that facilities are available to meet your needs.

CLWYD

●*Prestatyn:*
Bridge Restaurant, Bridge Road. Tel (0745) 855588
Brydots Coffee Shop, High Street. Tel (0745) 853365
Express Cafe, 29 High Street. Tel (0745) 853978
●*Rhuddlan:*
Town & Country Restaurant. Tel (0745) 590724
●*Rhyl:*
Barbican Restaurant, East Parade. Tel (0745) 342796
Fathom Restaurant, West Parade. Tel (0745) 337075
Flamingo Restaurant, 86 High Street.
Tel (0745) 342657
Rita's Cafe, Queen Street. Tel (0745) 353047
Shepherd's Cafe, Queen Street. Tel (0745) 351328
●*St Asaph:*
Barrow Cafe, High Street. Tel (0745) 582260

MID GLAMORGAN

●*Porthcawl:*
Atlantic Hotel, West Drive CF36 3LT.
Tel (0656) 715011
●*Bridgend:*
Heronston Hotel, Ewenny Road. Tel (0656) 668811

SOUTH GLAMORGAN

●*Cardiff:*
Chapter Arts Centre, Market Street, Canton.
Tel (0222) 396061
Ferrari's Baker, 33 Wellfield Road, Roath.
Tel (0222) 460355
Great British Burger, 1 St David's Centre,
Working Street. Tel (0222) 345179
Harvester's, Llanedeyrn, nr Cardiff.
Tel (0222) 549866
Heron Marsh, Cyprus Drive, St Mellons, nr Cardiff.
Tel (0222) 770700
Cardiff Moathouse, Llanedeyrn, nr Cardiff.
Tel (0222) 732520
Louis Restaurant, 32 St Mary Street.
Tel (0222) 225722
Old Orleans, 18-19 Church Street.
Tel (0222) 222078
Pizza Hut, 28 High Street. Tel (0222) 371557
Quayles, 6 - 8 Romilly Crescent, Canton.
Tel (0222) 341264

St David's Hall, The Hayes. Tel (0222) 342611 (various levels with buffet and bar facilities and Llandaff Celebrity Restaurant)
Wimpy, 14 St John Street. Tel (0222) 395000

There are also various accessible restaurant facilties in the following shopping complexes and department stores in Cardiff:

Capital Exchange, Queen Street
David Morgans, The Hayes
Debenhams, St David's Centre
Howells, St Mary Street
Littlewoods, Queen Street
Queens West, Queen Street

WEST GLAMORGAN

●*Port Talbot:*
Aberavon Hotel, Aberavon Beach, Aberavon.
Tel (0639) 884949
●*Swansea:*
Barn Restaurant, Cefn Velindre Farm, Mynydd Gelli Wasted, Pontlasau. Tel (0792) 774411
Dolphin Hotel, Whitewalls. *(entrance from hotel)* Tel (0792) 650011
Grand Theatre Restaurant, Singleton Street.
Tel (0792) 467387
Inn On The Lake, Singleton Park, Mumbles Road.
Tel (0792) 298023
Kardomah, Morris Building, Portland Street.
Tel (0792) 652336
Ladbroke Hotel, Pheonix Way, Llansamlet.
Tel (0792) 790190
Osborne Hotel, Rotherslade Road, Langland.
Tel (0792) 366274
Pastificio, 52 The Kingsway. *(Park Street entrance)* Tel (0792) 645473

GWENT

●*Chepstow:*
Huntsman Hotel, Shirenewton NP6 6BU.
Tel (0291) 7521
●*Cross Keys:*
Ynys Hywel Countryside Centre, Cwmfelinfach.
Tel (0495) 200113
●*Newport:*
Fratellis, Caerleon Road. Tel (0633) 264602
McDonalds, High Street. Tel (0633) 244947
Pizza Hut, Bridge Street. Tel (0633) 216335
Scarletts, High Street. Tel (0633) 253027
Wimpeys, Commercial Street. Tel (0633) 216822

GWYNEDD

●*Benllech:*
Bay Court Hotel, Anglesey. Tel (0248) 852606

Golden Sands Restaurant, Anglesey.
Tel (0248) 852384
Rhostrefor Hotel, Anglesey. Tel (0248) 852347
●*Betws-y-Coed:*
Plas Hall Hotel, Pont-y-Pant. Tel (0690) 6206
●*Blaenau Ffestiniog:*
Mwfanwy's Licensed Restaurant, 4 Market Place LL41 3NH. Tel (0766) 830059
●*Conwy:*
Clemence Restaurant, Castle Street.
Tel (0492) 593248
●*Llandudno:*
Alexandra Hotel, 1 Clonmel Street. Tel (0492) 76670
Ambassador Hotel, Grand Promenade LL30 2NR.
Tel (0492) 76886
Bodysgallen Hall, nr Llandudno. Tel (0492) 584466
Craigside Manor, Colwyn Road, Little Orme.
Tel (0492) 545943
Habit Tearooms, Mostyn Street. Tel (0492) 577993
Ocean Lounge, Canolfan Conwy, Promenade.
Tel (0492) 879771
Tribell's Fish Restaurant, 15 Mostyn Avenue.
Tel (0492) 75926
●*Llandudno Junction:*
Old Station Hotel & Beefeater Steakhouse,
Conway Road LL31 9NE. Tel (0492) 581259
●*Llanfair P G:*
Carreg Bran Country Hotel, Church Lane,
Anglesey. Tel (0248) 714244
●*Llangefni:*
Nant-Yr-Odyn Art Centre & Hotel, Llangristiolus,
Anglesey. Tel (0248) 723354
●*Llanrwst:*
Chandlers Brasserie, Trefriw. Tel (0492) 640991
●*Pwllheli:*
Lion Hotel, Tudweiliog LL53 8ND. Tel (0758) 701244

POWYS

●*Brecon:*
Bishops Meadow Motel, Hay Road LD3 0TL.
NB. Men's toilet not accessible by wheelchair.
Tel (0874) 2051
●*Crickhowell:*
Ty-Croeso Hotel, Dardy NP8 1PU. Tel (0873) 810573
●*Doldowlod:*
Argoed Mill Post Office & Tea Gardens, Doldowlod,
nr Llandrindod Wells. Tel (0597) 89234
●*Llandrindod Wells:*
Bells Country Inn & Gourmet Restaurant, Llanyre LD1 6DY. Tel (0597) 3959
Llanerch Inn, Waterloo Road. Tel (0597) 2086

Mostyn Hotel, Temple Street LD1 5HW.
Tel (0597) 2388/2120
Severn Arms Hotel, Penybont LD1 5UA.
Tel (0597) 87244/344
The Spinning Wheel, 5 The Spa Centre, Station
Crescent. Tel (0597) 3082
● *Llanwddyn:*
Lake Vyrnwy Hotel. Tel (069173) 692
● *Ystradgynlais:*
Mimosa Cafe and Restaurant, Commercial Street
Tel (0639) 842322

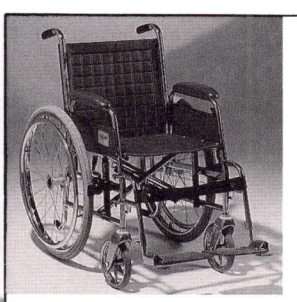

National key scheme toilets

Public toilets often leave a lot to be desired in any case and it is not unknown for toilets for disabled people in hotels and other buildings to be used as store rooms. The National Key Scheme is intended to ensure that there is a usable toilet nearby in most major towns. Keys for toilets fitted with the National Key Scheme lock can be bought from local authorities, the Royal Association fo Disability and Rehabilitation or the Wales Council for the Disabled (see list of useful organisations) or will be available at nearby premises. A full list of NKS toilets in Britain is available from RADAR. Toilets fitted with the NKS lock in Wales include:

CLWYD

- *Abergele:* Bee Field Car Park
- *Cefn-Mawr:* Tŷ Mawr Country Park
- *Cilcain:* Community Centre
- *Colwyn Bay:*
Central Promenade
Dingle Promenade
Douglas Road
Ivy Street Car Park
Lansdowne Road
- *Connah's Quay:* High Street, A548
- *Dyserth:* Waterfall Road
- *Holywell:* Gateway Car Park
- *Llanddulas:* Llanddulas Beach
- *Llansannan:*
- *Mochdre:* Station Road
- *Mold:*
Crosville Bus Station, Chester Street
New Street Car Park
Loggerheads Country Park, nr Mold
- *Old Colwyn:* Beach Road
- *Prestatyn:*
Barkby Beach
Bus Station, Ffordd Pendyffryn
Council Offices, Nant Hall Road
Ffrith Beach
The Nova Centre, Central Beach
- *Rhos on Sea:* Cayley Promenade
- *Rhuddlan:* Princes Road
- *Rhyl:*
East Parade
Barbican Bowling Green
Grange Road
Botanical Gardens
High Street
John Street
Town Hall
West Parade, Coliseum
- *Ruabon:* High Street
- *St Asaph:* High Street, nr bridge
- *Saltney:* Community Centre, A483
- *Shotton:* Alexandra Street
- *Wrexham:* General Station

DYFED

- *Aberaeron:*
North Beach
Pen Cai
- *Aberporth:*
Headlands Toilets
Penbryn Beach
- *Aberystwyth:*
Castle Grounds
Marine Terrace
Mill Street Car Park
- *Ammanford:* Carregamman Car Park
- *Broad Haven:* Car Park
- *Cardigan:* Chancery Lane

NATIONAL KEY SCHEME TOILETS

●*Carmarthen:*
Carmarthen Park
John Street Car Park
Priory Street
Provisions Market
St Peter's Car Park
Carmarthen Station
●*Cilgerran:* Playing Field
●*Clunderwen:*
●*Crymych:*
●*Cynwyl Elfed:*
●*Dale:*
●*Dinas:* Nr School Playing Field
●*Dre-Fach Felindre:*
Nr Newcastle Emlyn,
Parc Puw
●*Fishguard:*
Car park at rear of town hall, access via Hamilton Street
Picnic Area, nr convent
West Street Car Park
●*Freshwater East:*
Beach near Lakeside Cafe (Easter-October)
●*Freshwater West:* Beach (Easter-October)
●*Goodwick:* The Promenade
●*Haverfordwest:*
Castle Lake
Riverside
St Thomas Green
●*Johnston:* Pope Hill
●*Kidwelly:* Bridge Street
●*Kilgetty:* Information Bureau
●*Laugharne:*
●*Letterston:* Square
●*Llanddowror:* The Square, Tenby Road
●*Llandeilo:* Crescent Road Car Park
●*Llandewi Velfrey, Narberth:* Penblewyn
●*Llandovery:* Castle Car Park
●*Llanelli:*
Bristol House Lay-By
Market
Town Hall Square
Traethfordd Beach Car Park
●*Llanpumsaint:*
●*Llansteffan:*
Car Park
Green
●*Manorbier:* Beach (Easter-October)
●*Meiniciau:* Nr Kidwelly
●*Milford Haven:*
Manchester Square
Market Square
●*Narberth:* Towns Moor
●*Nevern:* Rear of Old School
●*New Quay:* Glanmor Terrace

●*Newcastle Emlyn:* Cattle Market
●*Newgale:*
●*Neyland:* Brunel Quay
●*Pembrey:* Country Park
●*Pencader:*
●*Pendine:* Caravan Site
●*Pembroke Dock:*
Hobbs Point
Market
Water Street, near library
Pembroke Dock Station
●*Porthclais:* Nr St David's
●*St Clear's:* Car Park
●*St David's:*
Bryn Road
Bishop's Palace
●*Saundersfoot:*
Coppet Hall (Easter-October)
Harbour (Easter-October)
Regency Car Park
●*Tenby:*
Castle Beach
South Parade
Upper Park Road
●*Velindre:* Nr Crymych
●*Whitesands:* Nr St David's

MID GLAMORGAN

●*Bridgend:*
Bus Station
Cheapside
Bridgend Station, Platform 1
●*Deri:* Cwm Darran Country Park
●*Maesteg:*
Car Park
Main Bus Station
●*Merthyr Tydfil:*
Bus Station
Shopping Centre, Dowlais
●*Pontypridd:* Station
●*Porthcawl:* Grand Pavillion

SOUTH GLAMORGAN

●*Barry:*
Broad Street, opposite Barry Hotel
King Square, behind Old Town Hall
Knap Car Terrace, Promenade West
Multi-storey Car Park, Holton Road/Court Road junction
●*Barry Island:*
Friars Road
Old Harbour Car Park (summer only)
Pavilion, Western Arcade, Paget Road

NATIONAL KEY SCHEME TOILETS

● Cardiff:
Central Square Bus Station
Llandaff Fields, Cathedral Road
Roath Park, Penylan Road
Roath Park, Rose Gardens
Victoria Park, Cowbridge Road East
Cardiff Central Station, subway
Cardiff Queen Street Station
● Cowbridge:
Market Place, The Butts
Town Hall Car Park
● Lisvane:
Cefn-Onn Park, Cherry Orchard Road
● Llantwit Major:
Boverton Road
● Penarth:
Albert Road
Esplanade Shelter, nr Lifeboat

WEST GLAMORGAN

● Fairwood Common: Swansea Airport
● Neath: Station
● Swansea:
Bus Station
Maritime Quarter, nr Lock Gates
Ravenhill Park
Quadrant Shopping Centre
Swansea Station, Platform 4

GWENT

● Abergavenny:
Castle Street Car Park
Old Bus Station, Monmouth Road
● Abertillery:
Tillery Street
● Blaenafon:
Big Pit Mining Museum
(museum hours)
● Blaina: High Street
● Brynmawr: Alma Street
● Caldicot: Car Park
● Chepstow:
Bank Street
Riverside
● Cross Keys: Gladstone Road/Risca Road Junction
● Ebbw Vale: Market Street
● Mitchel Troy: Picnic Site, A449 northbound
● Monmouth: Cattle Market
● Newbridge: High Street
● Newbridge-On-Usk: Picnic Site A449
● Newport:
Commercial Street
Kingsway Centre, 'In-Shops'

Newport Provision Market
Newport Station, Platform 2
● Risca: Tredegar Street
● Usk: Maryport Streeet Car Park

GWYNEDD

● Aberdaron: Nr Beach (May-September)
● Aberdovey: The Wharf
● Bala:
The Green
Plassey
● Bangor:
Dean Hill Car Park
Kyffin Square
Tan y Fynwent, near Bus Station
● Beaumaris: Nr Castle
● Beddgelert: Village Centre
● Benllech: Car Park, opposite garage
● Betws-y-Coed:
Cae Llan Car Park, off A5
Pont y Pair Car Park, off A5
● Blaenau Ffestiniog: Diffwys Car Park
● Caernarfon:
Castle Hill
Poolside Car Park
Turkey Shore
● Conwy:
Bodlondeb
Castle Visitor Centre
Morfa Beach Car Park
Quay
● Criccieth:
Esplanade (May-September)
Maes Car Park
Rear of Marine Terrace (May-September)
● Deganwy: Level Crossing
● Dolgellau: Marian Car Park
● Dolwyddelan: Adjoining Post Office
● Harlech: Bron y Graig
● Holyhead: Swift Square Car Park
● Llanberis: Bypass
● Llandudno:
George Street
Great Orme Summit (Interpretive Centre hours)
Happy Valley Road
Llanrhos Cemetery
Mostyn Broadway Coach Park
North Shore, nr paddling pool
West Shore, Dale Road Cafe
Llandudno Station, off Concourse
● Llandudno Junction:
Osborne Road Car Park, off A55
● Llanerchymedd: Market Square
● Llanfairfechan: Promenade nr Pavilion Cafe

NATIONAL KEY SCHEME TOILETS

●*Llanrwst:*
Gwydyr Park
Kwik Save Car Park, off A470
Watling Street Car Park
●*Llithfaen:* (May-September)
●*Menai Bridge:* Uxbridge Square Car Park
●*Mynytho, Pwllheli:*
Foel Gron Picnic Site (May-September)
●*Nantgwynant:* Pont Bethania (May-September)
●*Nantmor:*
Picnic Site, Aberglaslyn (May-September)
●*Nefyn:* Village Centre, off Pen-y-Bryn
●*Penmaenmawr:*
Fernbrook Road Car Park, off A55
Promenade, Underspace Toilets
Promenade, West End Toilets
Station Road Car Park (June-September)
●*Penrhyndeudraeth:* Car Park
●*Porthmadog:* Y Parc, High Street
●*Pwllheli:*
Y Maes
Penlan Street Car Park
●*Trawsfynydd:* Village Car Park
●*Trefriw:* Singrig Gardens, off B5106
●*Tywyn:*
Cinema
Recreation Ground
●*Valley:* Council Car Park

POWYS

●*Caersws:* Bridge Street
●*Clywedog Reservoir:*
Bwlch y Gle Car Park, South side of Lake
●*Knighton:* Norton Arms Car Park
●*Lake Vyrnwy:* Near Dam
●*Llandrindod Wells:*
Station Crescent
Llandrindod Wells Station
●*Llanfair Caereinion:* Bridge Street
●*Llanfyllin:* High Street, opposite Car Park
●*Llangynog:* Car Park
●*Llanidloes:*
Great Oak Street, behind Town Hall
The Gro
●*Machynlleth:*
Maengwyn Street Car Park
Y Plas Car Park
●*Meifod:* Car Park
●*Newtown:* Gravel Car Park
●*Welshpool:*
Berriew Street Car Park
Church Street Car Park

Llyn Cregennen, Gwynedd.

Information, Advice and Assistance

Whether you are travelling in Wales on holiday, business or visiting friends, there may be occasions when you need help with a specific issue. General information and advice agencies such as Citizens Advice Bureaux may be able to help.

Citizens Advice Bureaux

These are sometimes accessible to wheelchair users, but access is often via a back entrance only opened by prior arrangement. All bureaux offer a telephone service, and some will arrange a home visit for clients unable to reach the office.

The following bureaux are reasonably accessible for wheelchair users:

CLWYD

●*Deeside:*
34a Chester Road, Shotton.
Chair lift. Tel (0244) 819553
●*Flint:*
65 Church Street. Tel (0352) 63187
●*Holywell:*
The Old Library, opposite Post Office.
Tel (0352) 711262
●*Mold:*
Town Hall, Earl Road.
Ramped back entrance. Tel (0352) 3520
●*Prestatyn:*
1 Nant Hall Road. Tel (0745) 855400

GWYNEDD

●*Bangor:*
Ffordd Gwynedd. Tel (0248) 352598
●*Dolgellau:*
Gwernog House, Eldon Square. Tel (0341) 423070
●*Holyhead:*
6 Victoria Terrace, Anglesey.
Back entrance. Tel (0407) 762882

POWYS

●*Machynlleth:*
25 Penrallt Street. Tel (0654) 703131

Other Citizens' Advice Bureaux may be able to offer telephone advice or personal visits. See the local telephone directory.

Disability Groups

For more specific information on disability issues, the following organisations offer telphone and personal advice and information.

●*Wales Council for the Disabled*
Tel (0222) 887325
●*Spastics Society - Helpline:*
Liam Watson. Tel (0222) 798633

●*Disability Welfare Rights Trust:* Bangor.
Tel (0248) 352227
●*North Wales Resource Centre for Disabled People:* Bodelwyddan. Tel (0745) 583910 ext 4609

DISABILITY GROUPS

●C.A.T.C.H. UP:
Coleshill Centre, Llanelli. Tel (0554) 776850

Each of the eight counties and some districts in Wales also have local associations which can offer advice and assistance and will have information on local disability events and activities. The following are staffed in daytime hours:

●Action Aid for the Disabled:
193 Upper Dock Street, Newport, Gwent NP9 1DA.
Tel (0633) 258212

●Blaenau Gwent Council for the Disabled:
Community Centre, Northwest Approach Road, Ebbw Vale, Gwent.
Contact: Mrs Hilda Barwell, Secretary.
Tel (0495) 309036

●Brecknock Dial-A-Ride/Brecon & District Disabled Club:
Rhyd Offices, Canal Road, Brecon LD3 7HN.
Contact: Mr J Price.
Tel (0874) 3884

●Cair - Monmouth Association for Disabled People:
Castle Farm, Raglan, Gwent NP5 2BT.
Contact: Mrs Vivien Jones.
Tel (0291) 690492

●C.A.T.C.H. UP, Dyfed:
Coleshill Social Centre, Llanelli, Dyfed.
Contact: Mr Keith Skivington.
Tel (0554) 776850

●Clwyd Association for the Disabled:
Clwyd Voluntary Services Council, Station Road, Ruthin, Clwyd.
Contact: Mrs E Snowden.
Tel (08242) 2441

●Gwynedd Association for the Disabled:
Gwynedd Voluntary Services Council, 2 Slate Quay, Caernarfon, Gwynedd LL55 2PB.
Contact: Mr R J Jones.
Tel (0286) 2626

●Islwyn Council for the Disabled:
Springfield Centre, Llanarth Road, Blackwood, Gwent.
Contact: Mr Mike Harper.
Tel (0495) 222127

●Mid Glamorgan Association of Voluntary Organisations:
Development Officer, Maritime Offices, Woodlands Terrace, Maesycoed, Pontypridd, Mid Glamorgan.
Contact: Mr S Kent.
Tel (0443) 485337

●Montgomery Association for the Disabled:
Powys Rural Council, Davies Memorial Gallery, The Park, Newtown, Powys SY16 2NZ.
Contact: Mr J Brown, Secretary.
Tel (0686) 626220

●South Glamorgan Intervol Disability Forum:
Shand House, 2 Fitzalan Place, Cardiff, South Glamorgan CF2 1BD.
Contact: Ms Sally Fowler, Secretary.
Tel (0222) 485722

In an Emergency

Health problems or equipment breakage can happen any time, and there is nothing worse than being stuck in a strange area not knowing the best source of help.

Health Services

General Practitioners and Dentists

The increasing number of new surgeries built to take large general practices, often with a range of other services, has improved access to general health services in recent years. However, GP and dental surgeries are still based in inaccessible premises in many areas. Most Community Health Councils in Wales now have files, and in some cases directories, of accessible GP and dentist surgeries. Most of these listed below will give information by telephone.

Community Health Councils in Wales

CLWYD

● *Clwyd North Community Health Council:*
HM Stanley Hospital, St Asaph, LL17 0RS
Contact: Mr Alan Challoner, Secretary.
Tel (0745) 583412

● *Clwyd South Community Health Council:*
9 Grove Park Road, Wrexham, LL12 7AA
Contact: Mr I L Roberts, Secretary
Tel (0978) 356178

DYFED

● *Carmarthen/Dinefwr Community Health Council:*
12 Lammas Street, Carmarthen, SA31 3AD.
Contact: Mr D Davies, Secretary.
Tel (0267) 231384

● *Ceredigion Community Health Council:*
5 Chalybeate Street, Aberystwyth.
Contact: Mr J R Evans, Secretary.
Tel (0970) 624760

● *Llanelli/Dinefwr Community Health Council:*
Town Hall, Llanelli.
Contact: Mr E A Griffiths, Secretary.
Tel (0554) 751253

● *Pembrokeshire Community Health Council:*
Picton House, 2 Picton Place, Haverfordwest, SA61 2LU.
Contact: Mr C M George, Secretary.
Tel (0437) 765816

MID GLAMORGAN

● *East Glamorgan Community Health Council:*
13 Gelliwastad Road, Pontypridd, CF37 2BW.
Contact: Mr C Barnaby, Secretary.
Tel (0443) 405830

● *Merthyr & Cynon Valley Community Health Council:*
2nd Floor, Hollies Health Centre, Swan Street, Merthyr Tydfil.
Contact: Mr B Williams, Secretary.
Tel (0685) 4023

● *Ogwr Community Health Council:*
General Hospital, Quarella Road, Bridgend.
Contact: Mr M Davies, Secretary.
Tel (0656) 645700

●*Rhymney Valley Community Health Council:*
Ystrad Mynach Hospital, Ystrad Mynach, Hengoed.
Contact: County Councillor C Hobbs, Secretary.
Tel (0443) 812290

SOUTH GLAMORGAN

●*Cardiff Community Health Council:*
St David's House, 15 Wood Street, Cardiff.
Contact: Mr M Davey, Secretary.
Tel (0222) 377407
●*Vale of Glamorgan Community Health Council:*
24 Broad Street Parade, Barry CF6 8AN.
Contact: Mr M Davey, Secretary.
Tel (0446) 744010/744035

WEST GLAMORGAN

●*Neath Afan Community Health Council:*
The Lodge, 67 Margam Road, Port Talbot.
Contact: Mrs H M Swift, Secretary.
Tel (0639) 887083
●*Swansea/Lliw Valley Community Health Council:*
Trinity Buildings, 42 High Street, Swansea.
Contact: Mrs S Taylor, Secretary.
Tel (0792) 654967

GWENT

●*North Gwent Community Health Council:*
Leven House, Lion Street, Abergavenny NP7 5NR.
Contact: Mrs E Barwood, Secretary.
Tel (0873) 5349

●*South Gwent Community Health Council:*
2 Emlyn Walk, Kingsway Centre, Newport NPT 1EW.
Contact: Mr E P Roberts, Secreatry.
Tel (0633) 215666

GWYNEDD

●*Aberconwy Community Health Council:*
3 Trinity Square, Llandudno.
Contact: Mr W Parry, Secretary.
Tel (0492) 78840
●*Arfon/Dwyfor Community Health Council:*
Bodfan, Ysbyty Eryri, Caernarfon.
Contact: Miss D E Jones, Secretary.
Tel (0286) 4961
●*Isle of Anglesey Community Health Council:*
8A High Street, Llangefni, Gwynedd LL77 7LT.
Contact: Mrs D W Shaw, Secretary.
Tel (0248) 723283
●*Meirionnydd Community Health Council:*
Beechwood House, Dolgellau.
Contact: Councillor E G Griffiths, Secretary.
Tel (0341) 422236

POWYS

●*Brecknock & Radnor Community Health Council:*
11 The Bulwark, Brecon.
Contact: Mrs W F Wood, Secretary.
Tel (9874) 4206
●*Montgomery Community Health Council:*
Ladywell House, Newtown.
Contact: Mr F A Humphreys, Secretary.
Tel (0686) 27632

Hospitals

As elsewhere in Britain, casualty departments are being 'rationalised' and fewer hospitals now offer round-the-clock comprehensive coverage. In some counties only minor casualty facilities are available and you may have to travel some distance to the nearest main casualty department. It is advisable to telephone in advance, if only to ensure that parking places are available.

Hospital Casualty Departments

NB. The Welsh for hospital is *ysbyty*.

CLWYD

●*Rhyl:*
Glan Clwyd Hospital, Bodelwyddan.
Tel (0745) 583910
●*Wrexham:*
Ysbyty Maelor Wrexham, Croesnewydd Road.
Tel (0978) 291100

Minor casualty facilities are available at the following community hospitals:

●*Colwyn Bay Community Hospital.*
Tel (0492) 515218
●*Denbigh Infirmary.* Tel (0745) 2524
●*Flint Cottage Hospital.* Tel (0352) 62215
●*Holywell Cottage Hospital.* Tel (0352) 713003
●*Ruthin Cottage Hospital.* Tel (0824) 22088

DYFED

●*Aberystwyth Bronglais Hospital.*
Tel (0970) 3131

MID GLAMORGAN

●*Aberdare:*
Aberdare Hospital, Cynon Valley. Tel (0685) 872411
●*Bridgend:*
Princess of Wales Hospital. Tel (0656) 62166
●*Caerphilly:*
Caerphilly & District Miners' Hospital. (Monday-Friday, 9am - 5pm). Tel (0222) 851811
●*Church Village:*
East Glamorgan General Hospital. Tel (0443) 20424
●*Merthyr Tydfil:*
Prince Charles Hospital. Tel (0685) 721721
●*Rhondda:*
Llwynypia Hospital. Tel (0443) 430081

Minor casualty facilities are available at:

●*Aberbargoed:*
Aberbargoed Hospital, Rhymney Valley.
Tel (0443) 821521
●*Maesteg General Hospital.* Tel (0656) 732732
●*Mountain Ash Hospital:*
Cynon Valley. Tel (0685) 872411
●*Redwood Memorial Hospital,*
 Rhymney. Tel (0685) 840314

SOUTH GLAMORGAN

●*Barry:*
Barry Community Hospital, Wyndham Street
(Monday-Friday, 10am-4pm). Tel (0446) 733372
●*Cardiff:*
Cardiff Royal Infirmary, Longcross Street.
Tel (0222) 492233

WEST GLAMORGAN

●*Swansea:*
Morriston Hospital, Cwmrhydyceirw.
Tel (0792) 702222
Singleton Hospital, Sketty (daytime).
Tel (0792) 205666

GWENT

●*Abergavenny:*
Neville Hall Hospital. Tel (0873) 2343
●*Chepstow:*
Mount Pleasant Hospital. Tel (0291) 22232
●*Newport:*
Royal Gwent Hospital. Tel (0633) 252244
●*Pontypool:*
Pontypool & District Hospital (9am - 9pm).
Tel (0495) 3211

GWYNEDD

Minor casualty facilities are available at:

●*Bangor:*
Ysbyty Gwynedd. Tel (0248) 37007
●*Blaenau Ffestiniog:*
Ffestiniog Memorial Hospital. Tel (0766) 831281
●*Dolgellau:*
Dolgellau Hospital. Tel (0341) 422479
●*Holyhead:*
Stanley Sailors' Hospital, Anglesey. Tel (0407) 2384
●*Llandudno:*
Llandudno General Hospital. Tel (0492 860066
●*Penrhyndeudraeth:*
Bronygarth Hospital. Tel (0766) 770310
●*Pwllheli:*
Bryn Beryl Hospital. Tel (0758) 612231
●*Tywyn:*
Tywyn Hospital. Tel (0654) 710411

POWYS

●*Llanidloes:*
Llanidloes & District General Hospital.
Tel (05512) 2121
●*Machynlleth:*
Machynlleth Chest Hospital. Tel (0654) 2266
●*Newtown:*
Montgomery County Infirmary. Tel (0686) 27722
●*Welshpool:*
Victoria Memorial Hospital. Tel (0938) 3133

Wheelchair Repair

Damage to a wheelchair, artificial limb or any other piece of equipment can be difficult to get repaired, especially in the more isolated parts of Wales. The Welsh Health Common Services (WHCSA), which administers the artificial limb and appliance service in Wales, publishes a list of approved wheelchair service agents but, given current policies of contracting out services to private agencies, this list can change frequently. The list at the time of publication includes:

DYFED

●*Llanelli:*
Man Ton Motors, Yspitty Service Station, Bynea. Tel (0554) 254450
●*Narberth:*
Ludchurch Autos, Greenacres, Kiln Park Road. Tel (0834) 861181

MID GLAMORGAN

●*Aberdare:*
Martin Bush, Unit 29, Hirwaun Industrial Estate, Rhigos. Tel (0685) 813780
●*Bargoed:*
M J Steele, Station Road Garage. Tel (0443) 831742
●*Bridgend:*
Geoff Brooke, Seadowns, Beach Road, Southerndown. Tel (0656) 880576
●*Porth:*
Transport Repair Services, Tynewydd Sidings, Aberhondda Road. Tel (0443) 686688

SOUTH GLAMORGAN

●*Cardiff:*
Baileys Disabled Services, Collingdon Road. Tel (0222) 480250

S & S Electrical Services, 40 Bryn Cyn, Pentwyn. Tel (0222) 733442
Percy Smith, 142 New Road, Rumney. Tel (0222) 791298
●*Cowbridge:*
Mobility Wales, 4 High Street. Tel (0446) 773394

WEST GLAMORGAN

●*Swansea:*
Segmain Haulage, Stoneleigh Garage, Brunant Road, Gorseinon. Tel (0792) 892819

GWENT

●*Newport:*
Ken Roberts Motors, 133c Caerleon Road. Tel (0633) 259397

GWYNEDD

●*Llandudno Junction:*
John Hughes Garage, High Street. Tel (0492) 81216
●*Llangefni:*
Mona Industrial Workshop, Industrial Estate, Anglesey. Tel (0248) 722990

Artificial Limb and Appliance Centres

Three Artificial Limb and Appliance Centres (ALACs) in Wales can arrange emergency repairs to wheelchairs and other equipment.

●*Cardiff Artificial Limb and Appliance Centre:*
Rookwood Hospital, Fairwater Road, Llandaff, Cardiff CF5 2YN. Tel (0222) 555677
●*Swansea Limb Centre:*
Morriston Hospital, Heol-Maes Eglwys, Morriston, Swansea SA6 6LG. Tel (0792) 795252

●*Wrexham Appliance Centre:*
31 Chester Street, Wrexham, Clwyd LL13 8AR. Tel (0978) 290300

Emergency wheelchair repairs are also undertaken occasionally by bicycle repair shops and garages if no approved service agent is available.

Wheelchair Hire

If you find yourself with an unrepairable chair or if you need temporary use of a wheelchair for any reason there are a limited number of organisations with chairs for hire. These include:

● *Aberdare:*
Martin Bush, Unit 29, Hirwaun Industrial Estate, Rhigos. Tel (0685) 813780.
Manual only.

● *Cardiff:*
Shopmobility Cardiff, Bridge Street Car Park. Tel (0222) 399355.
Electric and manual chairs for shopping in Cardiff; manual only for longer term hire.

● *Cowbridge:*
Mobility Wales, 4 High Street. Tel (0446) 773394.

● *Cwmbran:*
Torfaen Community Enterprises Association, Caradoc Road. Tel (0633) 362951.
Electric and manual chairs for shopping in Cwmbran; manual for longer term hire.

● *Newport:*
Ken Roberts Motors, 133c Caerleon Road. Tel (0633) 259397.
Manual only.
Shopmobility Newport, 193 Upper Dock Street. Tel (0633) 258212.
Electric and manual chairs for shopping in Newport.

British Red Cross Society County Branches

Some Red Cross branches will loan or hire wheelchairs and other equipment for short term use. Contact the county branch for further details.

CLWYD

● *Red Cross HQ:*
Victoria Avenue, Prestatyn. Tel (0745) 852696.

DYFED

● *Red Cross:*
16 Spilman Street, Carmarthen, SA31 1JY. Tel (0267) 237874.

MID GLAMORGAN

● *Red Cross House:*
18 Pentrebach Road, Pontypridd, CF37 4BW. Tel (0443) 493333.

SOUTH GLAMORGAN

● *Red Cross:*
Murrayfield, St Fagan's Road, Fairwater, Cardiff, CF5 3XR. Tel: (0222) 569558/553195

GWENT

● *Red Cross:*
35 Stow Park Circle, Newport, NP9 4HF. Tel (0633) 267131/2

GWYNEDD

● *Red Cross House:*
Oxford Road, Llandudno, LL30 1DH. Tel (0492) 77886 (mornings only)

POWYS

● *Red Cross:*
5 Severn Square, Newtown, SY16 2AG. Tel (0686) 626663

Artificial Limb and Appliance Centres and the County and District disability associations may also be able to advise on sources of equipment for hire or loan.

Helpful publications

An increasing number of local and national authorities in Wales have produced guides to facilities for disabled people. The following have been useful in compiling this directory and can provide more detailed advice or information on accessible facilities.

●*Holidays in the British Isles, A Guide for Disabled People.*
RADAR (Royal Association for Disability and Rehabilitation), 25 Mortimer Street, London W1N 8AB

●*The Countryside and Wildlife for Disabled People.*
RADAR (Royal Association for Disability and Rehabilitation), 25 Mortimer Street, London W1N 8AB

●*Spectators' Access Guide.*
RADAR (Royal Association for Disability and Rehabilitarion), 25 Mortimer Street, London W1N 8AB

●*AA Guide for the Disabled Traveller.*
AA, Fanum House, Basingstoke, Hants RG21 2EA

●*On the Move: A Motorist's Guide for the Disabled Traveller.*
RAC, P.O. Box 100, South Croydon CR2 6XW

●*Easier Motoring for Disabled Drivers: Directory of facilities available at Shell garages,* Shell UK Oil, Shell-Mex House, Strand, London WC2R 0DX

●*Reservoir Recreation with Special Interest to the Disabled.*
Welsh Water, Lands and Leisure, Llyn Brenig, Cerrigydrudion, Corwen, Clwyd LL21 9TT

●*Information for Visitors with Disabilities,*
National Trust, 36 Queen Anne's Gate, London SW1H 9AS

●*National Key Scheme Guide, Accessible Toilets for Disabled People*
RADAR (Royal Association for Disability and Rehabilitation), 25 Mortimer Street, London W1N 8AB

Local Guides

●*Guide to Facilities for the Disabled on Anglesey.*
Isle of Anglesey Borough Council, Peyrorsedd, Llangefni, Anglesey, Gwynedd LL77 7JA

●*Guide for the Disabled, Colwyn District/Glyndwr/Alyn & Deeside.*
Clwyd Association for the Disabled, c/o Clwyd Voluntary Services Council, Station Road, Ruthin

●*Disabled Visitor Supplement.*
Tourism Unit, Aberconwy Borough Council, Town Hall, Lloyd Street, Llandudno

●*Directory for Disabled People.*
Llanelli Borough Council, Town Hall, Llanelli, Dyfed

●*Disabled Visitor's Guide.*
Arfon Borough Council, Town Hall, Bangor

●*Pembrokeshire Coast National Park: A Guide for Disabled Visitors.*
County Offices, Haverfordwest, Dyfed SA61 1QZ

Useful organisations

The following organisations are referred to in the guide or may be able to provide useful information.

● *Wales Council for the Disabled (WCD).*
Llys Ifor, Crescent Road, Caerphilly,
Mid Glamorgan CF8 1XL. Tel (0222) 887325

● *Spastics Society Wales.*
3 Links Court, Links Business Park, St Mellons,
Cardiff, South Glamorgan. Tel (0222) 797706

● *Sports Council for Wales.*
Mrs Marilyn Godfrey, Development Officer,
Sports for Disabled People, National Sports Centre,
Sophia Gardens, Cardiff, South Glamorgan.
Tel (0222) 397571

● *Arts for Disabled People in Wales.*
Ms Rhian Davies, Channel View Leisure Centre,
Jim Driscoll Way, Grangetown, Cardiff, South
Glamorgan. Tel (0222) 377885

● *PHAB (Physically Handicapped and Able
Bodied) Wales.*
Mr Gwynne Liscombe, Development Officer,
179 Penarth Road, Cardiff, South Glamorgan.
Tel (0222) 223677

● *Wales Council for the Blind.*
Ms Vanessa Webb, Shand House, 2 Fitzalan Place,
Cardiff, South Glamorgan. Tel (0222) 473954

● *Wales Council for the Deaf.*
Mr Norman Moore, Maritime Offices, Woodlands
Terrace, Maesycoed, Pontypridd, Mid Glamorgan.
Tel (0443) 485687 Minicom: (0443) 485686

● *MENCAP in Wales.*
169 City Road, Cardiff, South Glamorgan.
Tel (0222) 494933

Three Cliffs Bay, Gower.

Accessible
Wales

Your comments and opinions on facilities for disabled visitors to Wales would be welcome. If you would like to comment on any facilities in Wales you have used, would like to add new information to the guide or would like to be featured in the guide please use this form to give us as much detail as possible.

NAME AND ADDRESS OF FACILITY _____

_____

_____

_____

_____ TEL _____

INFORMATION ABOUT THE FACILITY - INCLUDE DETAILS OF ACCESS _____

_____

_____

_____

_____

READER'S NAME _____

ADDRESS _____

_____

_____

Please return this form to: Wales Council for the Disabled, Llys Ifor, Crescent Road, Caerphilly, Mid Glamorgan CF8 1XL.